Marillion

in the 1980s

Nathaniel Webb

sonicbondpublishing.com

Sonicbond Publishing Limited

www.sonicbondpublishing.co.uk

Email: info@sonicbondpublishing.co.uk

First Published in the United Kingdom 2020
First Published in the United States 2020

British Library Cataloguing in Publication Data:
A Catalogue record for this book is available from the British Library

Copyright Nathaniel Webb 2020

ISBN 978-1-78952-065-1

The right of Nathaniel Webb to be identified as the author of this work
has been asserted by him in accordance with the
Copyright, Designs and Patents Act 1988.

Typeset in ITC Garamond & ITC Avant Garde

Printed and bound in England

Graphic design and typesetting: Full Moon Media

DECADES | Marillion in the 1980s

Contents

Introduction

One of the great pleasures of writing about a cult band is meeting other people who are as obsessed as you are. Until I began work on this book, I had only one person to talk to about Marillion: my friend Andrew, who loves 'Grendel' so much he taught himself Anglo-Saxon and translated *Beowulf*.

Otherwise I was alone.

I discovered Marillion via my brother, an avid reader of rock reviewer Glenn McDonald, who for twenty years wrote a column called *The War Against Silence*. On 7 September 2000, McDonald published *TWAS #293*, an essay titled 'Chalk Hearts,' in which, inspired by the recent release of *The Singles '82-88'*, he spent 4,500 words comparing all fourteen versions of 'Kayleigh' then extant.

Here, thought my sixteen-year-old self, was something worth obsessing over.

At Bull Moose in Portsmouth, New Hampshire I picked up a CD called *Kayleigh*, which I thought was maybe the album the song was from but turned out to be a Dutch singles compilation from the mid-nineties, presumably made as a quick cash grab. It didn't matter, though: it opened with a seventeen-minute monster epic called 'Grendel' and the eight songs that followed were as drunkenly romantic as McDonald's strange essay had promised.

I was hooked.

Marillion are a cult band in nearly every sense, especially for American fans. Their records sold well in Britain throughout the eighties but they barely registered in the States. Meanwhile, the band has been dismissed or mocked by most mainstream pop gatekeepers, who crowed in 1981 that progressive rock was long since dead and buried and ought to stay that way, ate their words over the next decade, then promptly decided that the group could be safely, if inaccurately, relegated to the one-hit wonders bin. Looking back, every one of Marillion's successes seems coloured with a note of surprise, as though nobody really expected things to go so well... with one grand exception: the fans.

The fans have always been a huge part of the Marillion story. The stories of the band's dedication to their fanbase are countless, ranging from the epic (bussing a crowd from Aylesbury to London to ensure Marillion's Marquee Club debut would be a success) to the prosaic (Fish and roadie Yatta carrying a disabled fan up a flight of stairs to attend a second-floor gig). Marillion fans have never backed down from a challenge. They've traded bootlegs, called radio stations, pressured record companies. Most notably, they invented internet crowdfunding... Marillion fans are also exceptional for their kindness. On this I can present my own copious evidence. *Market Square Heroes*, the 1987 biography by Mick Wall of *Kerrang!*, proved hard to find and I ended up splurging on a band-autographed copy listed on eBay by an Englishwoman not far from Marillion's hometown of Aylesbury. A question about transatlantic shipping costs quickly became a conversation about music and Marillion, and I discovered that Kathy was an Aylesbury native who'd grown up with the band and had stories from every stage of their history. When my book arrived from the UK, it was packed with a veritable Christmas stocking of goodies from Kathy's nearly 40 years following Marillion and Fish.

Next I had to parse the huge collection of Marillion bootlegs – sure sign of a fierce and fearless fandom – to identify those of historical and musicological importance and, hopefully, hear them. This proved nigh-impossible, as bootleg sites are plagued with dead links, inaccurate labels, paywalls, and at least one piece of malware that I still haven't fully eradicated.

I'd nearly given up hope when I stumbled upon a website called Skyline Drifter, named for an early Marillion tune and dedicated to the massive collection of Mark Abbott and Peter Goodfield. (The Marillion bootleg community adheres to a few commendable rules, chief among them to never, ever share anything that can be purchased legally. This is a request directly from the band that the fans respect with admirable strictness.) A week after I first reached out, Mark had provided me with nearly nineteen gigs of history.

Slowly I made my way along the web of connections that comprises Marillion's magnificent fanbase. I spoke with Andre Kreutzmann of Marillion Setlists 1980-1988, a database of not just setlists but photos, tickets, posters, fanzines, and other memorabilia. I hunted down Claus Nygaard, author of the manuscript *In Shades of Green Through Shades of Blue*, which catalogues every gig played by Marillion until Fish's departure. Claus put me in touch with Jon Collins, who wrote the excellent Marillion bio *Separated Out*. I interrogated Stef Jeffery Depolla, the original *Web* mistress; Mark McCormac, holder of probably the best Marillion collection in the world; and Tim Glasswell, keeper of The Rainbow Room, a chronicle of Steve Hogarth's pre-Marillion bands. I learned from Jerry van Kooten, Claude Micallef Attard, Piet Spaans, and Stephan Brüninghoff. I talked drummers with the father of the bride at the wedding of a woman named Kayleigh (one guess at the father-daughter dance!). I even reached out to Mick Wall.

Every one of these people received me with the utmost grace and kindness. Jon dug out and photographed his original notes for me; Andre hunted down and debated demos; Mark identified an obscure poster (*very* quickly) and shared classifieds from *Melody Maker* and *Musicians Only*. Even Mick kindly replied that no, he didn't still have the notes for a book he'd written 35 years ago on a typewriter.

I offer great thanks to fellow rock nerds Jesse Young and Brian Kelly, chart guru TJ Murphy, and guest editor Chris McLeod. As always, I owe much to my wife, Molly, my son Jack, and the rest of my extended family. But this book simply must be dedicated to all the Marillion fans who've bestowed so much time and energy on a band whom the mainstream would happily have written off before they even started. So to Andrew, Kathy, Mark & Peter, Andre, Claus, Jon, Stef, Mark, Tim, Jerry, Claude, Piet, Stephan, Kevin, Mick, even Glenn McDonald: *I.O.U. for your love*.

And to the rest, welcome... it's a party!

Nathaniel Webb
Portland, Maine
April, 2020

Prologue: Silmarillion

It started with an engagement.

Just before Christmas 1977, the drummer for rock band Electric Gypsy proposed to a young woman from the tiny village of Brill in Buckinghamshire, England. Their love story cost the Gypsies their drummer, but the soon-to-be-bride was distressed to think of her fiancé's throne standing empty. In fact, she'd often heard someone practising drums in a shed next door to her father's house on Brae Road...

Mick Pointer, age 21, was a local kid who'd founded a hard rock band called Stockade in 1975. Beneath shoulder-length, centre-parted blonde hair he had the open face of the quintessential British working-man rocker, equally at home frying up fish and chips or onstage with Iron Maiden. After two years with no success, Stockade had split in the summer of 1977, leaving Mick to play his drums (and a bit of flute) alone in his parents' coal shed while working as a cabinet installer.

Introductions were made, an audition was held, and Mick got the gig. It should have been a good fit. The band played heavy, spacey rock, and Hawkwind had been Mick's first concert back in 1972. Also, he was immediately close with Gypsy bassist Doug Irvine – 'We just hit it off together musically, our ideas and how we wanted things to be', Mick recalled. '[H]e was like my soul mate, really.' But Mick wasn't satisfied.

Luckily, neither was Doug.

For starters, the rhythm section was more serious about music than the others. Per Mick, 'They spent less time doing music, and a lot more time talking crap and smoking dope all day.' Nor did Electric Gypsy's style satisfy the pair. Like Mick, Doug was a dedicated Rush fan, and they wanted to mix orchestral complexity with straight-ahead rock as the Canadian trio had done.

So in early 1978, Mick and Doug quit Electric Gypsy to form their own band. Through friends they met keyboardist Neil Cockle and guitarist Martin Jenner, and the foursome began writing and rehearsing instrumental music inspired by Rush as well as less radio-friendly seventies prog like Camel and Genesis. Through autumn and winter of 1978 and into 1979, they practised mostly at Mick's house, a ramshackle and unwelcoming place by all accounts, but remembered for a book that Mick noticed on the shelf one day while the band sat around debating possible band names: *The Silmarillion*.

The truth is that nobody in the group had read J.R.R. Tolkien's dense tome of myths and histories for the imaginary world of Middle-Earth, setting of *The Hobbit* and *The Lord of the Rings*. But they liked the name, enough for Doug to paint it boldly on his bass guitar case, and it stuck.

On 22 April 1979, the fledgeling Silmarillion had their only gig, at the Hambrough Tavern in the west London suburb of Southall. They opened for a punk band called Robert and the Remoulds, whose drummer worked with Neil and Martin, and despite this unlikely pairing, the show was a success in Mick's opinion: 'I remember playing to a small handful of people at this gig,' he said, 'and amazingly the most unlikely people were enjoying it... we were rehearsed, but not well-rehearsed. Just the first gig of any band and we were bashing away and playing, and these people were enjoying it. Just people with tattoo's [sic] drinking their beers, clapping "very good lads, very good." I'll never forget that gig.'

Any happy memories were overshadowed the next day, when a protest against a Southall meeting of the fascist National Front party led to a riot that resulted in the death of anti-fascist activist Blair Peach at the hands of the Metropolitan Police. The Hambrough Tavern itself would burn down some two years later during another skinhead-induced riot.

These early Silmarillion days had a lasting impact on the Marillion yet to come. A number of beloved tracks had their genesis in the long instrumentals Mick cooked up with his bandmates, notably 'Grendel,' 'He Knows You Know,' 'The Web,' and 'Garden Party.' Said Mick, 'You listen to the drum parts – they came first.' Silmarillion even made rehearsal tapes at a practice studio in Amersham, but these are long since lost, taken by Doug upon his departure in 1980.

Silmarillion attempted a few more gigs, but Martin soon grew frustrated with the band's lack of progress. He felt they needed to add a proper singer and get out of the rehearsal room, but his bandmates were slow to acquiesce. 'We started auditioning soon after the gig and tried some, I thought, very good vocalists,' the guitarist recalled. 'Doug and Mick were not happy with them, seemingly knowing exactly what they wanted. It was this slow forward motion to accept a vocalist and get out playing regularly that helped me decide to leave the band.'

Silmarillion did take on one permanent addition during this period, though, in the form of sound engineer Christopher 'Privet' Hedge. The band often borrowed a PA system from friend John Borlase, but nobody was much good with it, Borlase included. Luckily, Privet had attached himself to the fledgeling Silmarillion as a roadie, and they soon learned that he could coax a better sound from the borrowed PA than the man who owned it. Thus began a career mixing for Marillion that lasted decades.

With Martin out, Silmarillion needed a new guitarist, so Mick and Doug placed an ad in the *Melody Maker* of 14 July: 'Silmarillion requires lead guitarist. Camel/Genesis style rock band. No junkies/timewasters.' (They'd also advertised for a vocalist the week before, to no avail.) Some twenty hopefuls auditioned, but none of them fit. Finally, on the morning of Sunday, 12 August 1979, a car arrived from the town of Whitby, 225 miles away.

'I had called, but they'd forgotten,' recalled Steve Rothery many years later, while Mick insisted, 'He just sort of turned up. We never knew he was coming... I remember me and Doug not knowing he was coming. And we could have been anywhere.'

Luckily, Mick and Doug were home, though asleep. Nineteen-year-old Steve, who'd got up at six to load up all his guitar gear and make the journey to Doug's house in Long Marston, woke them up and insisted on having his audition whether they remembered him or not: 'I'd just driven two hundred and fifty miles to do this audition, so for them to get out of bed seemed fair enough!'

The soft-spoken young guitarist, baby-faced under a shaggy mop of black hair, began by playing them his demo tape, which mixed his own Hendrix-inspired riffs with the Beatlesy tunes of a singer-songwriter he'd been supporting around Whitby. Doug and Mick weren't impressed – Steve himself has since admitted the tape wasn't very good – but he'd come all this way, and had all his gear, so he convinced the pair to let him set up and show them what he could really do.

What they heard astounded them. 'He was very impressive,' Mick recalled. 'We sat there and watched as he played to us, and we gave him the job there and then.'

Steve arrived fully formed with the arpeggiated riffs and liquid, diatonic leads that would soon become his signature. Though a fan of the many progressive rock bands who drew from classical and jazz music, Steve himself developed surrounded by simpler sounds. 'I grew up in a little fishing village town near Whitby in North Yorkshire, England, and one of the big things there was an annual folk festival,' he recalled. 'So I kind of absorbed some of that, I suppose, in my musical identity. A lot of what I do comes more from a traditional English folk background than blues or jazz or classical, for example.' The folk fingerprint on Marillion is widely evident, from the finger-picked intro to 'Grendel' to the use of simpler harmonies than their prog predecessors in the band's long vamps.

A week after his audition, Steve returned to Long Marston to play with the band again and cement the decision all around for him to join up. He never left. Mick recalled that after his first audition, Steve 'stayed for the night and then drove back the next day, and then came back a couple of days later and stayed... Yeah, he just moved into the house, and we had a guitarist. So the three of us, it was Doug's house, and all three of us were living in this house together.'

Accounts differ as to when exactly keyboardist Neil Cockle left Silmarillion, but it was around this same time. Like Martin Jenner, Neil was frustrated by the band's inability to land either a singer or steady gigs, but more than that, there was an ongoing fight over ownership of (or perhaps financial responsibility for) the band's finicky Mellotron keyboard. As Mick tells the story: 'We had an argument with [Neil] about the Mellotron. There was an argument over money... I can't remember exactly what the argument was, but I remember the Mellotron coming back one night, and with silence [he] handed it over to us.' Steve recalled the split with Neil occurring on the very day he moved south: 'We turned up for a rehearsal, the second time I'd been down from Whitby, to find Neil's car, full of Doug's keyboards unlocked and with nobody around. After a blazing row between Neil, Doug and Mick we were a three-piece!'

The three-piece spent the next month and a half rehearsing but lacked adequate material for a live show. By October, they'd decided that they'd benefit from bringing a keyboard player back into the fold, so Doug reached out to a local keyboardist named Brian Jelleyman (who is cursed to have his surname misspelt 'Jelliman' in nearly everything written about the band thanks to an error in an early press kit).

Brian joined up, bringing a Farfisa organ and an Octave Cat synth with him as well as strong technical musicianship. Bassist Pete Trewavas, who would join up in 1982 after Jelleyman was gone, had known him in school and recalled, 'He'd had classical lessons and I think he was Grade 8 – he was good.' The addition of a second melodic and harmonic instrument gave Steve the freedom to experiment with his signature lead melodies, and the group quickly cooked up a strong set of prog rock instrumentals.

All four worked day jobs as well. Steve went through a few, including one making aluminium panels at a caravan factory that he promptly quit after a co-worker had a finger sheared off by the machinery. Brian had a steady position clerking at the nearby Aylesbury unemployment benefits office, a role that would inspire a few famous lyrics from Fish upon his arrival two years later.

But for now, the line-up of Doug, Mick, Steve, and Brian got down to work, writing and rehearsing. Despite the drastic line-up changes the band still had ahead of them, much of Marillion's style and sound was born in these days. The long, structured, multi-part instrumentals developed in late 1979 and early 1980 would yield riffs, changes, and entire sections destined for canonisation on *Script for a Jester's Tear* in 1983.

But first, Silmarillion had to get a gig.

1980: Professional Outlook Required

As the eighties dawned, Silmarillion were still in the rehearsal room. The line-up of Mick, Doug, Steve, and Brian – all with full-time jobs – split their practice time between an old music shop and the Queens Head pub in post-World War II 'new town' Hemel Hempstead, which Brian described as 'the main venue for band meetings.'

It was during this period that Doug took on vocal duties in an attempt to add excitement to the instrumental set that had yielded such little success thus far. He would prove an unsatisfying singer, but the change focused Silmarillion's writing and spurred much of the material that would survive to Marillion's debut album. With a set together, the band would soon begin gigging, but first, they wanted to get their new music on tape.

Also, the band agreed that the membership shake-up rated a name change. Mick recalled it as memorialising the loss of two members: 'When we did the split, I suggested to Doug that every time somebody leaves we should get rid of the bit of the front of the name, so that's why "Sil" went.' Steve was also concerned about the band name being taken so directly from Tolkien, both for the impact it had on the band's image and the possibility of legal action on the part of the author's estate. Whatever the cause, the name change was effected easily enough, recalled Steve: 'Doug had Silmarillion painted on his guitar case – all he had to do was paint out the Sil.' When exactly this happened is unclear – sometime between Jelleyman joining and the band's first gig – but it was late enough that on 1 March 1980 *Melody Maker* included a misspelt listing for a 'Silmerillion' gig on the 8th!

So Marillion set off for Hertford and a studio called The Lodge, founded and run by The Enid, an instrumental prog band who had released two albums on Marillion's future label EMI. The dates of the various 1980 demo sessions are unclear, but many of the recordings survive thanks to the band's dedicated and bootleg-happy fanbase. This first attempt was played straight to a two-track tape recorder at The Lodge and consists of five tracks: 'The Haunting of Gill House,' 'Herne the Hunter,' 'Scott's Porridge,' and two takes of 'Alice,' the first Marillion song to include vocals. (There was also, apocryphally, a demo made of 'The Tower,' an epic that was recycled into 'Grendel,' but no known recording survives.) While none of these songs lasted in the forms given on these demos, they provided bits and pieces to later tracks during the Fish years.

'Alice'

The session produced two versions of 'Alice.' The reason is immediately apparent – the intro to the first take includes a couple of drumming flubs by Mick – but there are also a number of differences between the performances. The song is mostly instrumental but does include a few lyrics inspired by *Alice in Wonderland*.

'Alice' opens with a power-chord progression in D-flat minor, then jumps to a double-time over which Brian and Steve play simultaneous leads. A hairpin turn leads into a harmonised line that itself gives way to a guitar ostinato over drum hits and big keyboard pads; Steve builds tension by using a delay pedal to harmonise with himself as the lead figure climbs up the scale.

'Alice' returns to the intro progression, this time with Steve playing a contrapuntal melody to Doug's vocals, which are muddy, out of tune, and buried so deep as to be almost inaudible. That guitar line was still in flux at this point; interestingly, the first take has Steve playing almost the exact part he would lay down two years later on 'Forgotten Sons,' while the second take features a less dramatic keyboard melody and only some simple harmonization on the guitar.

There are a few other differences between takes – the second version is lengthened by an extended outro full of noodling – but in the end, it was the fate of 'Alice' to be stripped for parts on behalf of a better song. Under Fish, 'Alice' became 'Snow Angel,' but ultimately its intro/outro progression was pulled (and rekeyed up a half step) for the long ending vamp of 'Forgotten Sons.'

'The Haunting of Gill House'

This gothic instrumental clocks in at seven and a half minutes, beginning with a sweeping synth glissando down to a held low note, a move that would reappear at the start of the early Fish-era song 'Charting the Single.' It bottoms out at a low D-flat, over which the bass meanders, the guitar plays echoing, dissonant chimes, and Brian adds Theremin-like wavering legato melodies.

After a minute, Doug gives a spoken-word recitation that's almost incomprehensible in the mix. The audible bits seem to include the phrases 'your house is burned to the ground' and 'But still, our very song gives rise to the legend of your house.' (Every bootleg calls the track 'The Haunting of Gill House,' and Fish calls it 'Gill House' as well when speaking of the version he did after joining, but the biography *Market*

Square Heroes has Steve refer to the song as 'The Haunting of Your House.')

With that spooky pronouncement, Doug enters with a repeating bass riff that pulses down the D-flat minor scale as the keys and guitar recontextualise it through a series of chord stabs, accented by cymbal crashes and rolling toms from Mick. Then Brian doubles the bass line with his right hand before everything fades away into a lone organ; this introduces a new, climbing bass line from Doug over which Steve plays his trademark swelling, delay-laden leads and the keyboard harmonises with the bass.

Another sudden stop heralds the change to a subtly swinging bass-and-drum groove that hints at Mick and Doug's Rush influence and allows Steve to take another short solo before the whole band crashes unexpectedly into the parallel major and Brian briefly plays a lead that later became the intro to 'Garden Party.' Then it's on to a double-time solo from Steve and Brian together, and just as suddenly back into half time and D-flat minor, melding back into that earlier swing for a final combined guitar-and-keyboard lead resolving into the dramatic last chord.

Overall, there's a lot to like in 'Gill House,' so it's no surprise that upon Fish's arrival it was given lyrics. The song became 'Silver Drifter' and then 'Skyline Drifter,' but ultimately it was scrapped – likely because it didn't fit the direction the band was heading – with the exception of the 'Garden Party' keyboard riff.

'Herne the Hunter'

Another lengthy instrumental, this time running over eleven minutes, 'Herne the Hunter' was the band's attempt at a 'folk legend,' per Steve – Herne the Hunter is a ghostly figure in English folklore, associated with Windsor Forest and Great Park in Berkshire. (He also featured on Marillion's first-ever T-shirts, self-produced in 1980.)

The song begins in A-flat minor with a majestic keyboard melody that suggests a hunter's horn. After about a minute the rest of the band joins in for a guitar solo and some keyboard improvisation around the original melody. This drops swiftly into quick synth arpeggios – suddenly in D-flat minor, apparently a favourite of early Marillion – that run over stabbing bass and drums, then climbing arpeggios over a martial rattle.

That section dies away into a watery synth played over a short bass melody, itself swiftly replaced by fingerpicked electric guitar that suggests the intro to 'Grendel.' A flute-like synth joins the guitar, creating a very seventies-prog mood. The return of the bass and the switching of the keyboard melody to a more organ-like tone builds the dynamics, then the song jumps into double-time with the return of the drums.

'Herne' meanders a bit, and some of the sections overstay their welcome, though there was material here for salvage if the band had wanted it. In 1981 the song kept its title while gaining lyrics from Fish, but it didn't survive long in the band's live set; they dropped it to prioritize the similar but superior 'Grendel' and nothing from it was recycled.

'Scott's Porridge'

Only a fragment of this track, about two minutes in length, survives, and there isn't much to it. It's a jam on 'Scotland the Brave' as played by Brian, which apparently arose during the band's early practise sessions, hence the alternate name occasionally given to the track, 'Scotch Porridge'. No doubt its Scottish patriotism appealed to Fish upon his arrival, because the jam was retained and extended (with the addition of another famous Scottish tune, 'The Bonnie Banks o' Loch Lomond') into the barn-burning encore 'Margaret.'

Satisfied with this record of their set, Marillion began gigging with a 1 March show at Berkhamsted Civic Centre in Hertfordshire. Brian recalled an uncomfortable debut: 'I know it was cold, as the fog from the dry-ice machine didn't stay on the ground where it was supposed to be.' Steve, at least, was warmed up by Privet's fledgeling pyrotechnics during 'The Haunting of Gill House,' recalling, 'One of the flashes didn't go off, so he scraped the contents into another one. When he let that one off, there was a huge sheet of flame up my back that nearly blew me off the stage. That was quite a first gig.'

Making matters worse, the crowd was 'less than fully receptive' by Marillion's own admission, though Steve and Mick have said that they made at least a few fans that day. One of these was a twelve-year-old boy named Steven Wilson who would grow up to be a prog-rock giant in his own right, known for his band Porcupine Tree and collaborations with such acts as Opeth, Dream Theater, and Yoko Ono, as well as four Grammy nominations. In Marillion-land, Wilson would co-write and produce Fish's 1997 solo album *Sunsets on Empire*, play guitar on the follow-up *Raingods with Zippos*, and helm a colossal 2017 remaster of Marillion's *Misplaced Childhood*.

Over the next nine months, Marillion played thirteen more gigs, most of them inauspicious: a Battle of the Bands, a Students Union of which Doug's girlfriend was president, a street fair that also featured a magician sticking six-inch nails up his nose, and a last-minute performance at a mental home in St Albans that was apparently expecting a cabaret band – the compromise was for Marillion to play a half-hour version of 'Johnny B. Goode' while the patients foxtrotted.

Undaunted – or perhaps inspired – by their limited success, Marillion set out to make a better set of demos, choosing tracks that featured tighter songwriting around Doug's vocals. In June they returned to The Lodge, only this time instead of playing live to a two-track tape, they went full multi-track. As with the first sessions, the exact dates of these recordings are a bit unclear, but two tracks survive: another version of 'Alice' and the new 'Lady Fantasy.'

'Alice'

The rerecorded 'Alice' hews pretty closely to the two earlier takes, so it's notable mostly for its vastly improved quality. The multi-tracking of course helps, but it's also clear that the band has benefitted immensely from their intervening months of practice and gigging. Mick's drumming is much tighter (and flub-free), Steve's guitar leads are confident and far less wandering, and the whole unit is much sharper and more professional than before. Far from the sloppy weekend-warrior vibe of the first demos, this take of 'Alice' showcases a band well on its way to professional status.

Doug's vocals are audible, as well, giving us what Steve later described as 'a really *nasal* voice, really quite awful if you want to know the truth.' The guitarist is being a bit unfair, but it's undeniable that one can almost hear how many takes it took to get an on-pitch vocal. (As Brian put it, the studio sessions were 'painful, trying to get Doug to sing in tune!') The lyrics, a few short stanzas of *Alice in Wonderland* references, are similarly not up to the later standards of Fish and Hogarth. Still, it's a test case that proved that Marillion's basic formula – vamping over a repeated chord progression while Steve plays melodic leads under a vocal – could work and work well.

'Lady Fantasy'

Perhaps the most retrograde of the Irvine-era songs is 'Lady Fantasy,' which is much closer to a pastiche of Rush's 1977 tracks 'A Farewell to Kings' and 'Xanadu' than the threatening, punk-influenced prog Marillion would soon develop.

Flat picked acoustic guitar and tootling Mellotron flute open the track, which swells with synths below and above, the latter taking their squeaky tone almost directly from mid-seventies Rush. For nearly two and a half minutes the song maintains a single mixolydian chord progression that appears all over inoffensive seventies rock (for example the acoustic intro to Bad Company's 'Feel Like Makin' Love,' in the same key of D). Doug's vocals – double-tracked for support – are in tune, but persist in delivering aggressively anonymous lyrics such as 'And my mind keeps on a-flyin', tryin' to be free/and my spirit comes to meet me/I'm as high as I can be.'

Eventually 'Lady Fantasy' delivers its first interesting moment as the diatonic major-key noodling is swept away by a towering wall of synth *ahhs* playing a D minor seventh underpinned by phased guitar chords. The moment quickly passes, however, as we drop into a very un-Rothery guitar solo over another set of tried-and-true seventies changes, this time a D-F-G-F not far removed from the D-F-C of Peter Frampton's famous 'Do You Feel Like We Do' jam.

The guitar solo fades into sweeping acoustic chords and more noodly synth playing a slight reimagining of the original progression; Doug delivers a final pair of verses over this altered form, which then repeats with a simple harmonised guitar lead until it fades away, not a moment too soon.

Under Fish, 'Lady Fantasy' got new lyrics as the Syd Barrett tribute 'Madcap's Embrace,' but the vocal melody is much the same, as though not even Fish could escape the tonal gravity of those old-fashioned changes. Indeed, 'Madcap's Embrace' didn't last long in the set, premiering at Marillion's first gig in 1981 and seeing only a few performances before retiring permanently in December of that year.

Mick later said that during this era, Marillion were 'a lot more laid back although the style was similar... It was more pretentious too. We would drag out an idea for about five minutes when it was really only worth about 30 seconds.' Harsh words, perhaps, but it's true that many of the songs that survive feature lengthy repetitions and unnecessary restatements. Perhaps they could have been cut down into tighter versions, but Marillion wouldn't get the chance: by the end of November, Doug had announced that he was out of the band and leaving music entirely.

Accounts differ of why Doug decided to quit Marillion, but one thing is certain: it came as a surprise. The group had been gigging recently and had just booked time at a studio in Gawcott called Leyland Hill Farm, intending to record another demo featuring their latest arrangements, when Doug broke the news. '[I]t was one of the biggest shocks of my life when he did that,' Mick said years later.

It might have been because of a woman – Mick once averred that Doug 'met this girl I think at a gig we did in High-Wycombe, and just disappeared' – but Doug may also have decided he'd grown too old for rock and roll. It seems Doug always had a cut-off date in mind; as Steve put it, 'Doug was the oldest member of the band and he seemed to expect things to happen for us too easily. He'd always said that if the band hadn't made it by the time he was twenty-five he'd quit. Then twenty-five came along and he did it – he quit!'

Doug's departure coincided with the late-November booking at Leyland Hill Farm, which nevertheless produced a single track featuring the ex-member's vocals. 'Close' would go on to be the most lasting piece of Irvine's legacy, just as soon as Fish got his hands on it.

'Close'

Today, 'Close' is best known for providing the basis for 'The Web' from *Script for a Jester's Tear*, but its original incarnation features some interesting musical developments over its nearly nine-and-a-half minutes. In some ways, it's a step backwards for Marillion, featuring a very seventies vibe both tonally and harmonically. Nevertheless, it features many Marillion hallmarks, such as fingerpicked electric guitar, melodic bass figures, and synth leads over big chord changes.

'Close' opens with guitar stabs that immediately put paid to Steve's rejection of any Rush influence: the riff, complete with echoing delay, is lifted almost verbatim from the overture of the Canadian trio's famous epic '2112.' The Rush pastiche is dropped quickly enough as the staccato hits give way to a smooth synth lead over which Doug sings a decidedly bland chorus: 'Any way, any how, all I need is you/if I told you in the night my lovin' is true/now you're gone, I'm so alone, well I have nothin' to do/ spend my time to remember, well I was close to you.'

The band drops away, replaced by chiming fingerpicked guitar from Steve, and Doug joins in for a verse. Mick's drums roll us back into the chorus – a terrific dynamic shift that demonstrates why this arrangement survived almost unchanged as 'The Web' – which again fades into a guitar-and-vocal verse, then another chorus.

This third chorus carries on into a guitar solo, somewhat unusual for

Steve as it eschews his usual liquid tone and melodic playing for a gritty, wah-pedal-heavy sound. It works, though, as the band beneath him, led by a huge bass tone from Doug, maintains the changes from the chorus but slowly alters their cadence until they're very nearly playing '25 or 6 to 4' by Chicago.

Eventually the guitar gives way to a restatement of the keyboard lead from the chorus, which then collapses back into synth pads and fingerpicked guitar. The bass and drums re-enter with a rolling, descending pattern, then this is rudely interrupted (in what sounds like an awkward tape edit) with a key change as a bright new synth lead enters.

This heralds the outro as first a galloping guitar, then more heavy bass-and-drum stabs, join the keys. Next, the rhythm section takes over the gallop as Steve plays slashing chords under a lengthy synth; then he returns to the riff that opened the section as the rest of the band hits the stabs together, renews the gallop, and finally joins the synth for a dramatic build-up that ends the track in crashing style.

Overall, 'Close' works quite well with the exception of the forgettable vocals, and indeed all it would take was the addition of Fish to make a successful track.

So Doug left music behind, taking the sole copy of an early Silmarillion demo with him. Mick, Steve, and Brian were stunned and briefly considered ending Marillion. To Steve, it 'came as a bit of a blow, especially to me as Doug and I had always been good friends.' Mick admitted, 'I must say, at the time I did feel like giving up, and I got to say, very much so, felt like giving up. 'Cause it was a major knock to me losing Doug, 'cause he was like my soulmate, really.'

Instead, the trio retired to the Queen's Head to regroup. A plan was swiftly hatched, Steve explained: 'Mick, Brian and I decided that *we* didn't want to call it a day, so we stuck another ad in one of the music papers.' On 6 December 1980, an ad appeared at the back of *Musicians Only*, chosen because there was no fee: 'Bassist, preferably with vocal ability required for established progressive rock group. Professional outlook required, but we play for love, not money! Own material. Aylesbury area. Genuine callers only.' Ads would continue under various wordings for the rest of the month.

Meanwhile, in a cottage in the Scottish Borders village of Ettrickbridge, two young men were spending their time dreaming of rock stardom and 'sitting in front of a two-bar fire zonked out of our brains listening to records at ridiculously high volume.'

That was according to bassist William Minnitt, called Diz, as in 'come here Diz Minnitt!' Seeking a new group to fill the hole left by the collapse of the pair's previous short-lived effort, the Stone Dome Band, they intended to place ads of their own in the music papers. They picked up a stack that included the most recent *Musicians Only*, where a certain ad caught Diz's eye. He promptly got Mick on the phone and pitched him on replacing Doug not with another bassist/vocalist, but one of each: 'Yes I can sing,' Diz said, 'but I happen to know this excellent singer who writes lyrics and is very much into acting and theatrics.'

That singer was one Derek William Dick, called Fish for his love of hours-long baths. Beneath a long mullet that would thin almost to nothing before he hit 30, the 22-year-old Scotsman was so massive that estimates of his height by overwhelmed acquaintances range from six foot four to six foot seven (the truth appears to be about six foot five and a half). A music fanatic from adolescence, Fish had decided only the year before to become a singer and discovered he possessed a voice of unanticipated delicacy and high register from such a huge frame. He'd sung his debut gig as recently as May, with Blewitt at the Golden Lion pub in Galashiels.

Diz and Mick swapped addresses, then demo tapes. Accounts differ on what, exactly, each demo contained. Steve recalled that Fish and Diz sent a recording of 'Fish singing along to a Yes number, though I can't remember which one, followed by him singing along to a Genesis track – "More Fool Me", a song that Phil Collins, *not* Peter Gabriel, sang on the *Selling England by the Pound* album... And there was a track on the tape of just him and the bass player doing something together.' Biographer Clive Gifford meanwhile claimed the tape included 'excerpts of Fish performing with his old band' – probably Blewitt, his band before the Stone Dome Band – 'and Diz with The Stone Dome Band. The cassette also contained lengthy spoken biographies and detailed analyses of the two Fish/Minnitt compositions that completed the tape. One was called "Crystal Epitaph", the other "Garden Party", both "arranged" for just one voice with bass accompaniment!'

In return, Marillion sent up a tape containing 'Close' and most likely 'Lady Fantasy.' It was mailed by Stef Jeffery, Mick's girlfriend and an early force in Marillion fandom, and part of her very funny accompanying letter of 10 December has survived:

Dear Derek + Diz (I think!?)
I'm writing this because nobody in the band can write – at least that's their excuse.
When you hear this, you'll understand why they've placed so much emphasis on the vocals!
We're hoping to lay down a tape with the present set on it to get to you before you come down. But this may not be possible as the old bassist has now refused to play through it with them and the tape made at the last gig did not come out (Basically because someone who shall remain nameless forgot to press the 'record' button!)
Anyway I hope this gives you a rough idea of the sort of thing we do...

Doug's much-maligned vocals notwithstanding, both sides found a lot to like in what they heard. Said Fish of his first impression of Steve, 'I thought fuck, this guitarist is brilliant. I've got to work with him.' He went on, 'To me, the tape had everything that I thought I could move into and contribute to the point that it would be a real band.'

Meanwhile, Marillion were iffy about Diz's bass playing but enamoured with Fish's voice. Steve remembered, 'Well, we sat there and listened to this tape and we all thought his voice was *brilliant*. He had the amazing ability to mimic Jon Anderson *perfectly* one moment, then Phil Collins, again *perfectly*, the next! We thought, this guy has got to be *it!*'

Despite their reservations about the bassist, Marillion understood that the pair came together or not at all, so they invited Fish and Diz down for a meeting that would take place on the first day of the coming new year.

1981: The Crying Jester

On 1 January 1981, Fish and Diz arrived at the squalid little house Steve, Privet, and roadie/PR man Guy Hewison (aged 21, Guy could rent a van) shared in Aston Clinton, a tiny village outside Aylesbury. They'd driven over 300 miles from the Scottish Borders in Diz's blue van – all their gear packed up and 'The Stone Dome Band' painted on the outside to give the impression of success – and gotten lost on the way, so it was no wonder the pair had no intention of returning home.

As Diz put it, 'They all came out, thinking that we'd come for an audition. We said, "Bugger the audition, we're here and that's that!"' First impressions were therefore rough; Steve remembered thinking of Fish, 'Oh, a big, loud, tall, arrogant Scotsman, just what I needed!' Luckily, the arrogant Scotsman had more to offer than just his attitude, as he'd come down with a new set of lyrics to 'Close' – now called 'The Web.'

There was no audition that first day; instead, the band shared a meal and a few beers at the house, then introduced their new members to the Rothschild Arms, a pub just down Weston Road. There, Fish and Privet got 'completely rat-arsed,' in Steve's words, 'and on the way back from the pub they both stripped naked, they were so pissed, and fell in a ditch.' Privet added, 'We walked back with no trousers on. It was all a bit weird and crazy.'

It was only uphill from there. On 2 January the fivesome repaired to Leyland Hill Farm, which had been rented for auditions, rehearsals, and recording. The studio, owned by local experimental folkie Wild Willy Barrett, was appropriately named as it resided in a converted stable – 'more Farm than Studio,' as Diz put it, 'with bales of hay and chickens in higher prevalence. When not gigging, the band's mikes, sound desk and multicore were in situ, enabling the "Studio" to function and in turn the band to have free space to rehearse.' Certainly, they hadn't chosen Leyland Hill for the convenience: Brian explained, 'The studio was in the lower part of the stable, with the mixing desk in the room above,' and Diz clarified, 'There was no direct connection with whoever was mixing. You couldn't see them.'

Nonetheless, the audition-cum-recording session was an immediate success. Fish, Diz, and the band jammed on 'Close,' 'Lady Fantasy,' 'Time for Sale,' and 'The Haunting of Gill House,' as well as a few shared influences, including Yes and the Genesis hit 'I Know What I Like (In Your Wardrobe).' The final test came when Fish put his vocals on tape for the first time by changing 'Close' into 'The Web' – an experiment that the singer later wrote 'made everyone realise immediately that we had something magical.'

'The Web'

The arrangement of this first demo is nearly identical to 'Close,' no surprise considering it's the same track (Diz didn't even replace the original bass, which was played either by Doug or possibly Steve after Doug quit.) There is a bit of additional synth, for example under the delayed guitar stabs that start the song, adding harmonic and sonic fullness. But the two big changes are a new guitar solo and the new vocal.

Steve keeps the wah pedal and some of the grit of his original take, but dials both back in favour of melodies strung together from long, soaring lines interspersed with quick bursts of shred. Many of the phrases in this version survived unchanged to *Script for a Jester's Tear*; overall, it's a much more 'Rothery' solo and suggests that losing Doug had already put Marillion on a road away from retrograde seventies influences.

Fish, meanwhile, proved himself immediately as both a vocalist and lyricist. Where Doug sang tentatively and as little as possible, preferring to leave long stretches of untouched instrumentals, Fish put words over nearly everything. From the first, his voice is full, confident, and tuneful. The pitchy moments are rare and never egregious, suggesting a singer who would have no trouble keeping on key in a live setting and getting spot-on takes in the studio. As well, critics who dismiss Fish as a mere imitator of Peter Gabriel and Jon Anderson might be surprised to hear how low this first version of 'The Web' is, with no falsetto and a melody that never even ventures beyond the G above middle C. Also missing, however, is the snarling grit Fish would soon uncover as Marillion added an edge to their sound.

The lyrics are also light years ahead of what Doug provided. Interestingly, 'The Web' maintains the theme of Doug's 'Close,' that of a recently-dumped lover who sits alone pining for his ex. But where the original delivered its story in bland seventies couplets, Fish tells a twisted version of the tale of Penelope, wife of Odysseus in the Greek Homeric epic *The Odyssey*.

'The Web' also marks the first appearance of a symbol that would define Marillion's early years. Fish was twenty years old and pumping gas at his father's garage the day Who drummer Keith Moon died, inspiring him to dream up a poem 'about even jesters crying – only a two-stanza thing.'

Fish saw Moon as the clown who makes audiences laugh despite his own sorrow, a powerful image that attached itself to Joseph Grimaldi in the nineteenth century, Dan Leno in the twentieth, and Robin Williams in the 21st.

But young, alienated Derek Dick had already associated the crying jester with himself. 'At school, I was very fat and people took the piss out of me, and that hurt,' he recalled. 'And I found that if you turn it around, you can take the piss out of yourself and make them laugh, and you immediately become a character. The jester.' In March 1980, the same month he failed an audition for Not Quite Red Fox, Fish put the crying jester to paper for the first time in a poem called 'The Allotment.' Scrawled on the back cover of Genesis's *Duke* for a friend, it ends, 'Will I savour the flower of fulfilment, or/Will I remain another crying jester caught forever,/in these brambles of malice.'

The band was instantly impressed by their new singer's way with words. 'I loved his lyrics straight away,' said Steve. 'I admit, I thought he could be a bit too wordy for its own sake, occasionally. But he was just a million times better than anyone we had ever come across before.' There was no question that Fish and Diz had the gig, and with a real singer and lyricist on board, all the work of the previous year was now fodder for reimagining. 'That night our dreams were charged,' Fish wrote, 'Steve and I sitting up till the wee hours going through the existing material and working through the possibilities of what we could salvage to create a brand new set.'

Ablaze with new energy, Marillion spent some ten weeks in rehearsals, splitting their time between the cottage in Aston Clinton, Leyland Hill Farm, and another studio called Anthony Hall. It was an extremely productive time, as Fish brought focus to the band's songwriting. (It helped that Fish, Diz, and Steve were all unemployed as well.)

'The Tower' became 'Grendel' thanks to Fish's heady lyrics based on the John Gardiner novel of the same name, a retelling of the Anglo-Saxon epic *Beowulf* from the monster's perspective. 'The Haunting of Gill House' became 'Skyline Drifter,' 'Lady Fantasy' became 'Madcap's Embrace,' 'Herne the Hunter' got lyrics, and 'Alice' became 'Snow Angel' (though later in the year it would be recycled into 'Forgotten Sons'). Even the 'Scotch Porridge' jam got a makeover, incorporating Fish singing 'The Bonny Banks o' Loch Lomond' in its evolution to a totally non-progressive but crowd-pleasing encore. The band also produced new material in the form of 'Garden Party' and 'Charting the Single,' plus a Rush-influenced

major-key instrumental called 'Time for Sale' that didn't last long.
The band's new focus wasn't all spent on writing, though. Despite an
awkward childhood, Fish discovered that 'aggressive band frontman'
was a role he could comfortably play. Diz recalled, 'When I first met him
he was still a bit self-conscious as he had been in another Progressive
band (Not Quite Red Fox), that hadn't given him a good experience. He
introduced himself as Derek rather than Fish. When we joined Marillion,
he used that as the opportunity to introduce himself as Fish and this
seemed to act as a catalyst to let him project a more self-confident part of
his personality.'

Or as Fish himself put it, 'I thought, right, I'm joining a band. All my
friends and my family thought that I was mad. It was a very hairy time.
I spent the next six months doing auditions, and then in 1981, I joined
Marillion. And because I'd given up so much I infected the rest of the
band with my enthusiasm. I never actually sat back and thought I was
going to fail. That may seem incredibly arrogant and big headed, but I
never considered failure. I knew it was going to happen. It was as if all the
confidence I'd never had when I was at high school suddenly reared up
and gave me this huge push.'

The result was that Fish promptly took over from Guy as the fledgeling
band's PR man as well. To this day, his bandmates give him the credit for
taking them to the next level. Diz recalled, 'Fish was the one who got
us all the best gigs. He was this walking PR machine and was just very
driven... [He] just grew in his confidence and would set himself targets
of getting gigs or chasing record companies, with sometimes surprising
results. I remember answering the phone one day to find Peter Gabriel
on the other end who had called to give us some positive feedback on the
first demo Fish had sent him.'

As Steve put it, 'We immediately became a lot more professional. Fish
was so ambitious, ruthlessly so. All the qualities that made him difficult to
work with also gave him his drive.' Guy agreed: 'Without Fish's pushiness,
the band wouldn't have had the measure of success it had. It probably
wouldn't have amounted to anything.' And lastly Mick: 'Certainly Fish had
a much more cue idea of publicity and marketing... He was a massive asset
in the start.'

Fish began with a goal in mind: a gig at the Friars, an Aylesbury music
promotion at the heart of the humming local music scene. But first
Marillion had to prove themselves at smaller shows, which they did with
gusto.

Fish's cold-calling bore fruit and the new line-up played their debut on 14 March 1981, in the backroom of a Bicester pub called the Red Lion. Sources disagree on the size of the audience; estimates range from fifteen to 30 to 65. But despite his nerves ('wetting himself he was so nervous,' said Steve) Fish rose to the challenge of fronting the band to a hostile audience. From the outset, he had face paint to protect him – 'Nothing very elaborate for that first gig,' Steve recalled. 'Just these two fish-eyes.' – but it was enough. 'I had the idea of putting on the painted mask to overcome my shyness,' Fish explained. 'If something went wrong, I could pretend it wasn't my fault. It was the guy in the mask and nobody would recognise me in the street without the make-up.'

Marillion played four more gigs that month, all within spitting distance of Aylesbury, and another five in April. Fish swiftly came out of his shell as a frontman. By their third gig in March the fish-eye makeup had become a full-face Union Jack; a week later he was wearing a cape and wielding a mic stand against a gang of skinheads trying to trash the venue ('He was rock-hard and scared the crap out of them,' recalled Privet.)

The end of spring also saw Fish forced to take on a day job for the first time since moving down. Brian found him a spot at Aylesbury's unemployment benefits office, where the singer would regularly arrive either hungover or still coming down from the previous night's excesses. One morning it was acid in Fish's system, Diz recalled: 'Some bloke came in to sign on while Fish was completely off his face. Instead of getting him to sign the form, he made him do four circles and six signatures on this piece of paper. The guy went home thinking that he had signed for his benefit.' Fish spent another morning scribbling the first lyrics to 'He Knows You Know' on the desktop to take his mind off terrible stomach cramps. Managing the dole also helped inspire the revolution anthem 'Market Square Heroes' – its original title was 'UB 2,000,001.'

The final piece of Fish's new life in Aylesbury was a fledgeling relationship with a pretty young pharmacist at Stoke-Mandeville hospital. 'I met her and went *wow*,' Fish recalled of the girl with the euphonious first and middle names of Kay Lee. Thus began an on-again-off-again love that would lead, in its roundabout way, to superstardom.

May picked up a bit with eight gigs, including Marillion's debut on the 29th at the Friars in its location at the Aylesbury Civic Centre on Market Square. The band and their singer had earned the notice of Friars manager David Stopps: 'Fish was a larger than life character. His presence was felt in the town as soon as he moved down.' Stopps invited them to support punk poet John Cooper Clarke, though Marillion would be tucked away in the smaller Aston Hall rather than Maxwell Hall where the headliners played. Les Payne, a local musician who would produce the band's first demo a month later, suggested they step up their costume game for the occasion. Undaunted, Fish headed to the Hammer House of Horror TV studio in Hampden Woods, which was closing down and selling off their massive collection. The singer came home with a full stage set for the Friars gig, including gravestones, dry ice, and monks' robes.

Unfortunately, it was not until the show had begun that Marillion discovered their robes were made of a fabric that was nearly translucent under the glare of the footlights. 'During the gig I turned around to see Diz,' recalled Steve. 'As I did, the lights came on and the material became transparent. So, there he was stood in his undies. I thought, well if I can see him... I couldn't help but feel a bit exposed after that.'

By then the setlist had shed nearly all vestiges of Doug Irvine's influence. Consisting of 'He Knows you Know,' 'Garden Party,' 'The Web,' 'Charting the Single,' 'Grendel,' and 'Margaret' the show was Fish all the way – and a huge success. The crowd began as a small knot of existing fans but drew in the mix of punks, metalheads, new wavers, and skinheads who comprised the Friars' regular audience. As Diz put it, 'The first Friars gig we did supporting in a side hall of the main venue saw us start the evening with a group of hardcore fans numbering less than 20 and by the end, we had well over 400 crammed into the room, and demanding more.'

Marillion suddenly realised they had something special on their hands. Diz recalled, 'I remember coming off stage and turning towards Steve and we both had these incredible maniacal grins on our faces, and there was this palpable sense of euphoria,' and later added, 'We were all close to tears at the end.' Privet agreed: 'It was a bloody amazing gig. One of those things where you don't realise how important it is until afterwards. More people came to see us than to see the gig in the main hall.'

Success was confirmed when a subsequent Friars newssheet said Marillion's back-room appearance was 'being talked about as one of the best live performances seen in Aylesbury this year.' It would also be the band's first contact with London manager John Arnison, who was managing John Cooper Clarke at the time and would soon take on Marillion as well. Fish had met his goal of a gig at the Friars and the band had risen to challenge.

June saw another increase in gigging, with eleven shows, including another distinct marker of success: repeat performances at earlier venues. They weren't all winners, though. The White Hart paid a pittance, and the second time around, the crowd consisted of a handful of surly drunks. The Horn of Plenty had holes in the stage covered by carpet. Fish fell through the floorboards at the Horse and Groom in Bedford. But Marillion took the gigs anyway and played them all like they were the Friars.

By July, Marillion had decided it was time to capitalise on their growing live success with two upgrades: a proper demo and a real PR man. Fish couldn't do *everything*, after all, however he might have tried. And the band was fearful of falling into the dustbin of history despite their strong showing thus far. As Fish told *Kerrang!* a year later, 'What's happened is that there were a lot of bands putting together good material, that just became totally disillusioned. They found they weren't getting the exposure needed to get people to gigs. We'd found that by July 1981, so we employed a PR guy, Keith Goodwin, to get our name in the papers, make sure we were always in the gig guide, and that way we got journalists, radio stations interested.'

If band legend is to be believed, Goodwin – a big name who'd managed the press for Yes, Black Sabbath, and Argent among others – wasn't given much of a choice in the matter. As biographer Claus Nygaard puts it, Fish 'just stormed into his office in London one day and almost forced him to be Marillion's PR agent.'

Meanwhile, David Stopps had introduced Fish to Les Payne, a local musician training as an engineer at Roxon Studio. On Saturday, 18 July the band trooped down to Watlington for a weekend session paid for by their gigging income. ('I think it was about £400 but Les gave us a deal,' Fish recalled.) Payne had only planned to produce, but when the engineer fell asleep at the desk, he stepped into that role as well.

The session went smoothly, and on Monday night, three final mixes were put down: 'He Knows You Know,' 'Charting the Single,' and 'Garden Party.' 400 copies of the tape were produced, intended for promotion and distribution to record companies, but by August fan demand led to it being sold at gigs and by mail as well.

The Roxon Tape
'He Knows You Know'
The demo roars to life with Marillion's punkiest track. This song took its final form on *Script for a Jester's Tear* and this arrangement is startling

for just how different it is. Thunderously reverbed drums summon dark power chords from the guitar, over which Fish spits out the opening lines with heavy delay. Halfway through the verse he switches to falsetto for the first time, but rather than the delicate, flutey sound he would later put to tape, here he achieves a taunting whine that captures the smug 'unwanted advice... from well-meaning people with no experience of the subject' as Fish later put it.

Brian's organ fills out the sound as the band crashes through the second verse, delivered with even more venom by Fish and enhanced by a dirty phaser. Then everything echoes away except a single muted bass with a nauseating slapback delay; over this, a gentle synth pad, and some guitar swells, Fish delivers the gentle chorus, which shifts from the song's A minor base to the parallel major in a comforting turn towards melodicism.

Then the band kicks back in for the loudest, wildest verse yet, aided by Steve's liquid leads, which dissolve into a brief solo before Fish nearly screaming out the final verse. The second chorus finally comes in as a whisper, but there's no safety to be found; rather than returning to the major-key changes of the first chorus, we stay in A minor and crash unexpectedly down to the totally non-diatonic F-sharp. This Black Sabbathy tritone progression carries us to the end, when Fish delivers one final 'you know!' drenched in reverb and delay.

'Garden Party'

The arrangement here is much the same as it would appear on *Script*, though it opens with some inoffensively jazzy electric piano from Brian over the sounds of glasses tinkling, corks popping, and Marillion and friends doing their best imitation blueblood chatter. The keys cut, Fish snootily asks for a drink, and then the familiar rising synth lead enters.

There are few differences after that, though Fish's delivery is a bit less polished – he's pushing too hard where he would later opt for delicacy – and there are some ill-advised contrapuntal vocals that were happily soon discarded. The keyboard solo is different as well, a result of it being Brian's rather than the later Mark Kelly's, and Steve's guitar solo has some choked-off phasing on it.

'Charting the Single'

This is a curious tune that went through a number of arrangements, all of which never quite made the cut. In this first incarnation, it's very hard rock, almost glam. The verses are driven by a chugging palm-muted guitar riff made up of all major chords in A mixolydian, but over them Fish delivers perhaps his most self-consciously punny lyric, a huge collection of food and drink wordplay that follows a philandering bachelor through his sexual conquests on the continent. (It's also, as the title suggests, a none-too-subtle hint that record companies might be wise to pick up this savvy new band.) The lyric was meant to be ironic – Fish called it a 'total piss-take of the male dream of fucking about' – but phrases like 'Schnapping my fingers on an alcoholiday' and 'get a pizza the action' just come off as goofy. As well, the words are often too much for the song, forcing Fish to cram them in over an inadequate framework.

The verse drops into a very Genesis little transition, pumping synth and bass raising the key for the half-time chorus, which recalls 'Lady Fantasy' and plenty of other seventies rock with its D mixolydian modality. The vocal is a little uncertain in this arrangement; there's no strong melody to hang onto as Fish gets through his words then repeats the title of the song a few times.

A breakdown follows, featuring a somewhat out of place synth solo (is it a rock song or a prog song?) and then, cleverly, the verse progression passes by once in the dominant key of E to return the song back to its root for the next proper verse. From there it's into a double chorus with extra lyrics and a final repetition of the title to close out the proceedings.

The Roxon demo was dutifully sent to all the labels in London, who rejected it out of hand – even EMI, who would sign Marillion a year later. Of course, as Fish would later delight in pointing out whenever possible, 'He Knows You Know' went on to hit #35 on the UK charts (and #21 on the Billboard Mainstream Rock chart in the US, a feat surpassed only by 'Kayleigh') and 'Garden Party' would reach #16. 'Charting the Single,' ironically, never charted.

Still, the tape was a hit with fans, it helped in booking gigs, and with the aid of Keith Goodwin, it earned Marillion a few inches in *Sounds*, who described them as 'an Aylesbury five-piece who freely admit the marked Genesis influence in both their writing and performance' but were kind enough to note how the tape could be purchased and mention some upcoming dates.

July saw only six shows and August only four, but one of those four was a big one: Marillion's return to the Friars, this time in the 1,250-capacity Maxwell Hall as support for the American band Spirit. David Stopps had invited them back, though as the bottom band on the bill Marillion had only ten minutes for a quick line check before their set began. This didn't stop them from pulling out all the stops at their biggest show yet. Fish broke open a ketchup-filled cucumber during 'Garden Party' and for 'Forgotten Sons' he used his mic stand as a rifle and crushed blood capsules in his mouth to dramatize the dead soldier of his lyrics. The result, just as their first time at the Friars, was a resounding success for Marillion. Many early fans still have fond memories of that night, but Stopps put it best: 'They are going to be big... They're one of the most exciting bands to come out of Aylesbury in the last few years. They took the place apart.'

The triumph won them more press attention. In addition to the *Sounds* mention Marillion scored a review in the local *Bucks Advertiser* celebrating their 'amazing reception from their followers in the Maxwell Hall.' And the dates kept coming, as Marillion realized they'd never get anywhere with the labels unless they arrived with an army of fans at their backs.

With Goodwin on board, the quality of Marillion's gigs generally increased. September saw the band take second billing to Welsh metallers Budgie at City Hall in St. Albans, where they'd previously been relegated to the Horn of Plenty and its dangerous stage. The next month, which saw the official launch of the Saliva Tears Tour, Marillion hit their next big milestone after the Friars: the Marquee Club in London, which would soon become their home.

The first Marquee gig, on 20 October, is recognized by everyone associated with Marillion as a major turning point. On the strength of their relentless self-promotion and positive notices from important venues like the Friars, Marillion were booked to support the now-forgotten hair rock act Girl, giving them a shot at opening up the all-important London gig market and the labels and managers who haunted it.

In keeping with tradition, the show threatened disaster but was saved by Marillion's penchant for over-preparation. They'd already set up a telephone hotline for fans to keep up on the latest gig news and now they leveraged their Aylesbury influence by hiring a bus to cart fans down the A41 to London, deviously ensuring a friendly audience.

And it was a good thing, too, as headliners Girl weren't too friendly themselves. Minnitt recalled that they 'spent absolutely ages setting up and sound checking so that we had virtually no time... I also recall them pretty much sabotaging the sound as well before we went on.' But Privet earned his stripes by quickly whipping the sound system into shape, 'and then the sense of elation as the crowd tuned in to what we were doing and Fish got well into his stride to great effect. At the end of the gig, Girl accused us of trying to sabotage their set up, which was a classic case of transference. I guess it was the fact that we went down better in front of what should have been their crowd.' And it was true, too, as Marillion earned an encore, a rare feat for a support act.

Fish remembers Girl as much more gracious, claiming that they 'had a good attitude about it, they gave us congratulations afterwards.' But Steve held onto an entirely different memory of Marillion's Marquee debut: 'the night we all decided Brian [Jelleyman] had to go.'

Long after the fact, accounts of why Jelleyman was sacked range widely. His playing is sometimes praised and sometimes derided, often by the same people. Biographer Mick Wall insists that the rest of the band found their keyboard player 'pigheaded and arrogant.' But one criticism is constant: he simply wasn't willing to commit to the band full time.

In Brian's own words: 'I never really put the practice in. I can understand the frustration Fish and the others felt at the time – I knew my attitude wasn't right. I knew the band was destined for success, but I couldn't become what was needed. Everyone needed to be as totally dedicated to the band as Fish was, and I wasn't.'

Brian hung around for a few more weeks of gigs, including a Halloween return to the big stage at the Friars, as Fish encouraged the band to scout out his replacement. On 11 November lightning struck when Marillion opened for a psychedelic group called Chemical Alice at the Electric Stadium in Chadwell Heath. Playing keys for Chemical Alice was a young Irishman named Mark Kelly. Tall and slim with thin lips, smouldering eyes and razor cheekbones, Kelly was bored out of his mind: 'The guitarist was into all this cosmic stuff from groups like Hawkwind. All he wanted me to do were silly synth noises.' Meanwhile, the opening band really seemed to have something going on: 'I watched their set and decided that I really wanted to play with them.'

Fish and Mick saw something special beneath the silly synth noises. Recalled Mick, 'I said to Fish, I remember we were standing together watching this keyboard player doing his stuff, and I said, fucking hell, you know, he was pushing his keyboard around, and he was dancing around, and he was only 19 at that time, and he hadn't been playing that long himself, but you know, his enthusiasm was for it.'

Fish, ever devious, struck up a conversation with Chemical Alice after the show and got the guitarist's phone number. He spent a few days trying to wheedle Mark's number from the unsuspecting axeman without arousing suspicion, and when he finally did, he called to tell Mark that Brian was out and he was in if he wanted it. As Mark recalls it,

[T]hey had said: 'Come and join the band, we're going to sack Brian', or Fish was saying all this. I'm like: 'Well, I don't know, really, because I'm at college', and he's going: 'Oh, you gonna have to move to Aylesbury'. I'm thinking: 'Great, I'd love to play in the band, but I don't know if I can quit college just like that'. So I said: 'Well, I'll think about it', and he said: 'Well, come and see us play again to help make your mind up.'

Brian played a few more gigs, including an extremely disappointing show at the 101 Club in Clapham where the audience was tiny and the venue charged for the PA. Then, on 20 November, Mick picked up Mark and his girlfriend from Chesham Station and brought them to Elgiva Hall, where Marillion were to play their 69th show, offering the job again on the way.

Mark saw two appealing motives for leaving Chemical Alice for Marillion. First, 'They seemed so professional to me – they clearly wanted to be successful.' And second, the singer of Chemical Alice had recently been dumped by his girlfriend, who promptly took up with Mark. Quitting Chemical Alice would neatly sidestep any drama, a fact very evident to the new item, who hadn't yet broken the news to the singer.

At the hall, Mark tried to make himself inconspicuous, but Brian 'knew something was wrong as soon as he saw me at Chesham. He recognised me and knew that something was going on. I was trying to keep out of the way...'. After the gig, Mark accompanied Fish home to Aston Clinton, where they stayed up all night talking and listening to music. The next morning Fish summoned the rest of the band and they went together to Brian's house to break the news: Mark Kelly had joined Marillion.

21 November was an auspicious day for another reason: the publication of Marillion's first gig review in a national music paper. Xavier Russell of *Sounds* had good things to say about the band's Marquee debut a month earlier: 'Marillion recently took London by storm, and gave Aerosmith rip-off merchants Girl a bit of a scare... Marillion have a very tight sound. Songs like "He Knows You Know", "Garden Party", and "Charting the Single" are all long workouts, well crafted, not too much guitar, and synthesizer drifting in and out. Fronting this rather complicated sound is Fish, who does have a good voice, and sings pretty off the wall lyrics.' He concluded, 'The sooner Marillion get signed, the better.' Mark had picked the perfect time to join up.

28 November saw Marillion play a single keyboardless show, then it was back to Leyland Hill Farm for intensive rehearsals prior to Mark's debut with the band at the Great Northern in Cambridge on 1 December. The old Mellotron, which had been band property since the days of Neil Cockle, was bequeathed to Mark. (It tended to chew up tapes, forcing Mark to strip it down and wash it before every gig in the shower at the Aston Clinton cottage where he moved in with Fish and Guy Hewison.) He also brought two keyboards of his own, a Yamaha CS-15 synthesizer for leads and a Farfisa Compact Duo organ.

'I didn't know any of the songs,' Mark recalled of the Great Northern gig. '"Grendel" was the main one. I had to write all the chords down to jog my memory.' He had no choice but to learn quickly, as Marillion were booked solid. 2 December was in Chadwell Heath. 3 December saw what should have been a triumphant gig opening for folk-rockers Lindisfarne, but the night was marred when Lindisfarne's sound engineer demanded that Marillion fork over a twenty-pound bribe to be allowed to play. 4 December likely washed away any bitter taste, though, as Marillion returned to Friars Maxwell Hall.

Mark's arrival was a sea change for the band's setlist, as the last vestiges of Doug Irvine-era songwriting were more or less washed away. As the keyboardist explained:

There were two or three other tracks that I didn't particularly like when I joined the band, 'The Madcap's Embrace' was one of them, and 'Skyline Drifter' was another one that I thought wasn't as good. They had given me tapes and stuff to learn the songs, and I only had a week to learn all the songs before we did the first gig, so I was panicking a bit, and I picked the ones I liked best, really, and left the others till last and never quite got round to learning to play them... So by me joining the band and not knowing the song, it was sort of like 'Oh, well we won't do that one, as Mark doesn't know it'. I thought 'never mind' cause I don't like it. So I never learned it, and we never played it again... So that's what happened to 'The Madcap's Embrace', 'Skyline Drifter', and 'Herne the Hunter' and all those others. 'Time for Sale', that was dreadful, it was Brian's instrumental.

A couple more gigs culminated in Marillion's Christmas Eve appearance at the Starting Gate in Milton Keynes, now something of a home base and a place to try out new material. For their 75th show and the closer to a year of colossal strides forward, the band debuted two new songs, including the first written with Mark's input. The soon-to-be-crowd-favourite 'Three Boats Down from the Candy,' which features an unforgettable keyboard lead in the second half, went over well. 'The Institution Waltz' didn't have as much impact and was retired not long into 1982. (Bootlegs survive of this song and it's easy to see why it never caught on, as it's quite simplistic and amelodic compared to the bulk of Marillion's output.) At last, the band rang in Christmas with an impromptu cover of 'I Know What I Like' by Genesis, Fish tossing in lyrics from other Genesis songs and even a snippet of the Kinks' 'Lola' as the spirit moved him.

1981 closed much as it had begun, with the injection of new blood bolstering Marillion's seemingly indefatigable drive toward success. The Friars Club annual poll saw them voted best local band and best support band as well as the sixteenth best show of the year, above such prog heavyweights as Camel and King Crimson. Indeed, David Stopps was forced to defend the Friars against criticisms that they were overbooking Marillion to the detriment of other local bands. He wrote, 'Any other band with anything like their level of determination, professionalism and following would have got the same treatment.' If other bands simply lacked those things, well, Marillion were always ready to take up the slack.

1982: Let the Blood Flow

1982 was the year it all came together.

There would be challenges, certainly, and a friendship would be destroyed much as Doug and Mick's had. But the year would ultimately go down in Marillion history as a string of triumphs, a carnival ride of ceaseless activity and apparently limitless growth that got underway as soon as New Year's had gone and never once let up.

'82 kicked off with a 3 January return to the Marquee for a second support gig, this time opening for a different now-forgotten metal band called Spider. Already, Marillion measured up to the act that they were purportedly just supporting: Spider had headlined the night before at Electric Stadium, where on the 7th, Marillion would do the same.

Marquee manager Nigel Hutchings felt the same way – impressed by Marillion's performance as well as their audience draw, he offered them a headlining spot only two weeks later. On the 25th, Marillion returned to the Marquee for the first of fourteen headline gigs in 1982.

The show was a success in more ways than one. Marillion had no trouble bringing in the crowd, but this time it was more about who was in it. Per the *Bucks Herald*, A&R men from Chrysalis, Polydor, and Phonogram were there, but most important was Tony Wilson, the producer of Tommy Vance's *Friday Rock Show* on BBC Radio 1. Wilson's girlfriend was Spider's manager, and unbeknownst to Marillion, had dragged him out to see the band that had outshone her own earlier that month. Wilson was suitably impressed and a *Friday Rock Show* session was booked for only four days later at the BBC studio on Delaware Road in London.

But first Marillion had to survive another Electric Stadium headline, where they came onstage to faint applause from a bored crowd. It was the perfect opportunity for Fish's charisma to prove how he and the band had converted audiences across England so swiftly. Catching the lack of enthusiasm, Fish promptly hissed, 'Shhh! One should always maintain silence in a morgue.' He then spent the gig tweaking Privet Hedge, first explaining that the soundman had requested a bit more acknowledgement of his hard work during shows, then pausing between each song to invite the crowd to say 'Hello, Privet!' again, and again, and again...

On the 29th, Tony Wilson met Marillion at the BBC studio to produce their *Friday Rock Show* debut. Only half a year earlier Fish had sent a copy of the Roxon Tape to the BBC hoping for a slot on the *Friday Rock Show* and been turned down via photocopied form rejection. Now here they were for Mark's first recording session as a member of Marillion – and Diz's last.

They played three songs: 'The Web,' 'Three Boats Down from the Candy,' and 'Forgotten Sons.' The hasty recordings exist somewhere between the studio and the stage, keeping their live arrangements and featuring little in the way of overdubbing, but sporting better sound than the bootlegs and demos that comprised Marillion's output thus far.

The *Friday Rock Show* appearance was a hit with Marillion's fans, who were in the midst of organizing themselves. Late February saw the publication of the inaugural issue of *The Web*, the semi-official Marillion fanzine that still exists today. Helmed by superfan Tim Hollings, *The Web* #1 featured three hand-written pages including the lyrics to 'Garden Party,' a band history, a clipping of the 1981 *Sounds* gig review, an exhortation not to miss the *Friday Rock Show* broadcast on the 26th, and most importantly, the Good Gig Guide that listed Marillion's tour dates through March. The Guide would become an essential part of Marillion's activities as it enabled fans to track the band's movements, ensuring a healthy reception wherever they toured.

The next day saw an equally momentous publication, a return to *Sounds* magazine in a two-page interview. March continued Marillion's newsmaking: they earned their first features in *Kerrang!* and *Record Mirror*, and on the 7th played their second Marquee headline. It was a sell-out – and another last for their bassist, who was on his way out.

Diz didn't know it. He recalled, 'I remember it being a really good gig, in common with all the ones we did at the Marquee, and we had a lot of record companies turning up at that point so there was quite a buzz around. As far as I can remember the relationship with everyone was good... it felt as though something was really beginning to roll and recognition was just around the corner.'

But the rest of the band weren't so sanguine, as Mark's arrival highlighted Diz's shortcomings. Steve explained, '[W]e were progressing so rapidly musically that whatever weak links we still had left in the band were really starting to show themselves.' Or as Fish put it, 'We couldn't have a band with passengers.'

Meanwhile Marillion had heard that Aylesbury pop group the Metros were close to breaking up. They were a trendy bunch, described to biographer Mick Wall as 'a sort of pop band that had gone through about half a dozen "image changes" in the search for success. The Metros were about cute make-up and long blonde wigs, you know?' But Fish caught a March gig of theirs anyway and discovered that their pretty-faced, diminutive bassist, Pete Trewavas, possessed remarkable talent – as well as a prog rock pedigree, having briefly played in the band Orthi.

The singer and bassist got to chatting after the show and Fish let Pete know Marillion were on the hunt for Diz's replacement. For his part, Pete was uncertain that prog rock offered much of a future, but was impressed by Marillion's work ethic. He requested an audition; Fish coolly agreed.

The time came after a mid-March gig at Birmingham University. Mark blames himself:

> Diz had gone up there, and his girlfriend had gone with him, and they decided to stay. We didn't have anywhere to stay, so we came back, and on the way back everybody was bitching about him like he wasn't there. And I said: 'You know, he's not really very good,' and it was like, 'Yeah, you're right, he's not, let's sack him.' So I'm like, 'Oh, my God, what have I done there?'

With Diz away, Pete came to the band house to audition. Marillion's first reaction was scepticism: 'I had very short, slightly red hair at the time,' recalled Pete, 'and I was wearing white trainers which was a bit of a no-no. They asked me what music I was into, I told them that I'd been listening to Haircut 100 and their eyes got wider and wider. If I'd said that I had a load of Caravan, Pink Floyd and Genesis in my collection, maybe they would have taken me a bit more seriously...'

But like Steve in 1979, Pete plugged in and auditioned anyway (after being told, 'You can use Diz's amp, he won't mind!'). 'We were so impressed by his tuning up that we gave him the gig then and there,' Mark recalled, only a slight exaggeration. The audition started with 'Garden Party,' and during the song Fish, Steve, Mark, and Mick locked eyes and knew: they had to have Pete.

All that remained was to give Diz the news. Accounts differ on how things came to a head, but it's certain that he was dumped just before a 26 March gig at the Starting Gate in Milton Keynes. As Mark tells it,

> [O]f course Fish was like: 'It's your idea, so you got to sack him, you're the one that have to do it.' ... First of all, I said: 'Do you think it's a good idea to tell him now just before a gig, cause it's bound he won't play,

he's gonna take his gear and go home, that's what I'd do.' Fish's going: 'No, he'll play.' I'm thinking 'No he won't,' so I thought... what I'll do is, you know, blah-blah-blah, trying to sort of break it to him gently. Fish is like: 'Oh, let me do this.' It's like, 'You're sacked and you're useless,' you know. I'm like: 'Oh God.' So, of course, he went home, and we ended up doing the gig just the four of us... I found it a bit scary, actually, cause I just thought, 'Well, I'll be in this band about a year and that will be it, 'cause Fish will probably get around to sacking me next.'

And Mick's version:

I got blamed for that. It had nothing to do with me at all, but the decision had been made to lose Diz... apparently he came to talk to me, and I seemed to be rather strange with him, and he seemed to think there was something wrong. But I never actually said anything to him, there was no reason why he should possibly think something was wrong anyway, and I never did find out actually who said what. But anyway, for some reason, Diz decided half an hour before the gig to tell us all to fuck off. So we played that night without a bass player. I think Fish was not happy about telling him. No, I remember being told at the time that for some reason Diz picked up something from me; I never said anything to him, but I had a strange attitude or something towards him.

Biographer Claus Nygaard theorizes that Fish's attempt to shift the blame onto Mick may actually have been a political move, a way for Fish to distance himself from the drummer who would be the next casualty in the band's tooth-and-claw struggle to improve. Certainly it was clear to all of Marillion that Fish had no trouble firing a friend if he felt it was what the unit needed.

However it happened, there was no doubt that Diz had to go. The bassist himself has come to agree: 'As an observer, I can see why they did it,' he said years later. 'My standard of musicianship and my style did not fit.' And the truth is that Marillion were right. The musicianship of the rhythm section improved immensely upon Pete's arrival, creating the line-up that would soon get signed, break into the singles chart, and record a masterful debut.

Pete's rehearsal trial-by-ordeal began the next day, 27 March, and he played his first gig with Marillion on 2 April at the General Wolfe Club in Coventry. This and a show in Scarborough a week later were just warm-ups, though, for the next phase of Marillion's assault on the big time: the Scottish tour.

April and May 1982 saw extremely heavy touring, with a show nearly every day beginning with their Scottish debut on 11 April. Fish had booked some 29 gigs in his homeland, and the long stretch away forced Marillion to take the plunge once and for all into professional musicianship – there was no keeping a job in Aylesbury now.

The band was a hit in Scotland. Their draw increased with each show and even the music press took notice. Not every review was favourable – Andrea Miller wrote in *Sounds* that Marillion 'sound like early Genesis without the wit' – but most were, including Phil Bell, also of *Sounds*, who wrote, 'Mark my words. Critics may choke and chuckle en bleeding masse. But when action's sizzling at grassroots level, to apathetically ignore it would be tantamount to dodging our duty.'

On 8 May Marillion returned south to continue gigging in England and Wales. They were feeling good. Privet confirmed the impact of the assault on Scotland, saying later, 'The enthusiastic anorak fan thing started on the Scotland tour. There were some lads from Luton who just kept showing up and the Scottish fans increased by the gig... After Scotland, I felt that we weren't playing at rock bands any more, it was a profession.' He added, 'It was about that time that I knew that the band was going to make it.'

All the burgeoning band needed now was a manager.

Their first choice was David Stopps, the Friars promoter who had said such glowing things about Marillion the year before. Fish had been pressing Stopps to take the role and in May he gave in. Stopps' work began by contacting sending copies of the Roxon demo to some fifteen record companies, as well as mailing out press kits and helping buy a PA system.

June was a quiet month, with only two shows, but one of them was Marillion's first headline at the Friars – making local history as the first unsigned band to do so. By July Stopps was making headway with two labels, EMI and Charisma. He'd first caught the attention of Tony Stratton-Smith, called Strat, the president of Charisma Records and the man who'd guided Genesis to stardom a decade earlier. Strat came to one of Marillion's Marquee headline gigs in late May, liked what he saw, and began scheming to bring the band on board.

Also at that Marquee gig was a man from whom David Stopps borrowed five pounds to buy Strat a drink: one John Arnison, erstwhile manager for such acts as Status Quo and Rory Gallagher, who had just set up shop on his own. He'd gone to the Marquee, a favourite haunt of his, to talk with Sony about signing John Cooper Clarke.

On stage that night was Marillion.

Arnison recalled,

> It was the first time, in fact, that I'd bothered to watch a band do their set the whole of the way through in months. And I was captivated! I'd never heard of them but the minute they came off stage, I ran over and asked Keith Goodwin if they had a manager. He said, 'Yes, Dave Stopps...' I thought, 'Oh no! I'm too late...'

Arnison told Goodwin, Marillion's press officer, 'Listen, you know my numbers, any help or advice, give me a call.' Luckily for him, Marillion were about to fire Dave Stopps.

They were good friends, but the fact was that Stopps couldn't give his all to the growing machine that was Marillion. His work for the Friars was too demanding, and while he intended to transition to the band full-time, it wasn't fast enough. 'We panicked,' Mark recalled, 'we thought he was being too relaxed and we were getting nervous.' Or as Fish put it, 'We became concerned that we'd put on an anchor rather than wings.'

So Stopps was out. Fish did the deed as usual, and Stopps was hurt enough that Marillion wouldn't play the Friars again until March 1983. But the loss of a major promoter didn't slow Marillion, as Fish promptly called John Arnison and said, 'I understand you'd be interested in managing us, do you want to meet?'

Also interested was Peter Mensch, who had worked with Ted Nugent, Aerosmith, and AC/DC, and was now managing a fledgeling Def Leppard. For his part, Arnison was certain Marillion would choose the bigger fish. But as Steve tells it:

> After Dave Stopps was gone, we decided it was down to either John Arnison or Pete Mensch to manage us. So we made an appointment to see them both. Peter Mensch took us to his house in London – very posh, gold albums all over the walls... But the thing that really struck us, I think, is that he was far more interested in getting hold of Fish's name on a management contract than he was in getting the rest of us to sign. Then we went to see John, who we met in a pub in Earls Court... He came across as a bit of a local rogue but ultimately somebody you could trust. John impressed us after Peter Mensch because he was so down-to-

earth by comparison. He was interested in making the band happen and, like us, he saw it all in terms of albums; we definitely didn't want to be a band that relied on a constant stream of hit singles, and he said he totally agreed with us on all that.

The band repaired to the pub bathroom for a quick huddle, where they agreed to offer Arnison the job – but they made him wait another two or three days before Fish called and said, 'Congratulations, John! You're the new manager of Marillion! That is, if you still want to be...?'

Arnison's first task was to manage negotiations with Charisma and EMI. Tony Stratton-Smith had been courting the band aggressively; Mick recalled of a 9 July show, 'I remember being picked up from a gig in Retford we did once by Tony Stratton-Smith, I think me and Fish, we had a ride back from the Midlands in a Rolls Royce... I remember the air conditioning in the car, and the armrests, and I was thinking "I can cope with this." You know, we drove there in a van smelling of piss, and we come back in a Rolls Royce.'

But Strat made a tactical error that soured things with Marillion. Eager to snag the band but staring down his own summer vacation, Strat sent his business manager with orders to sign Marillion by any means necessary. The underling, unimpressed with what he saw, offered a measly contract for two singles.

Geffen Records was also interested at the time, as were Phonogram and Atlantic. Geffen got as far as a preliminary sit-down, but as Steve put it, 'That fell apart when we realised they were talking about cutting all the songs down to three minutes long! We dispensed with the idea of signing to them *very* quickly when we found that out.'

Meanwhile, EMI was making moves of its own. A&R man Ashleigh Goodall asked Marillion to record some demos for them as a sort of proof of concept prior to a proper record deal. Goodall left EMI soon after, but nevertheless on 26 July the band headed to the basement of the EMI building in Manchester Square, London to spend two days with producer Danny Dawson, putting down new versions of 'Market Square Heroes,' 'He Knows You Know,' and 'Chelsea Monday.' (The latter two are included on the bonus disc of the 1997 remastered edition of *Script for a Jester's Tear*.)

The band weren't too keen on the results, nor was John Arnison. So the manager pitched a new plan to Goodall's replacement, one Hugh Stanley-Clarke: EMI senior execs would come see Marillion on their home turf at a packed and ebullient Marquee headliner in early August. Steve recalled,

'When he saw what was going on down there, Hugh told John he definitely wanted to sign us. He saw that the Marillion audience wasn't a load of old '70s rock fans there for a nostalgic night out. It was young kids coming to see us... our audience's average age was from between about fifteen and eighteen. Seeing us at the Marquee really swung it for us with Hugh.'

On 25 August, Marillion and EMI agreed to terms on a contract that would soon be signed. The next night the band dedicated their gig in Liverpool to John Arnison, who had made it all possible. But the official announcement would have to wait a few more days.

The 28th saw Marillion's first big festival appearance, playing Theakston's Music Festival in support of Jethro Tull. The show was nearly a disaster: as Ian Anderson looked on from the wings, the band struggled with a dead keyboard and a mismiked guitar amp, resulting in silence from both Mark and Steve. It was a good thing, though, as it served as dress rehearsal for the big time: the Reading Festival on 29 August.

Reading was a traditional step up for Marquee favourites, and despite their low billing, Marillion blew the crowd of 35,000 away, earning two encores. Most of their set was broadcast on BBC Radio One, and 'He Knows You Know' and 'Three Boats Down from the Candy' soon marked the band's first official appearance on vinyl as their performances were included on the *Reading Rock Volume One* LP of live cuts from the weekend.

The other history-making moment at Reading was when Fish, buoyed by the enthusiastic crowd and brimming with enthusiasm, announced from the stage that Marillion would be signing with EMI. Tony Stratton-Smith was flabbergasted, having assumed that his business manager had done as he asked and won the band for Charisma. Horrified, Strat promptly made a deal with John Arnison for Charisma to handle Marillion's publishing. Per Arnison, 'He immediately wrote out a cheque for five thousand pounds, and said, "Whatever you get offered from anybody, I'll pay that plus five thousand."'

He also fired the business manager.

On 6 September Marillion headed to Fair Deal Studios – per Mark, 'a small and inexpensive studio in a shed at the bottom of somebody's garden' – to cut another demo for EMI, this time in preparation for the first single. Producing was David Hitchcock, who had helmed Genesis's *Foxtrot* among other seventies prog heavyweights. On the menu that day were 'Market Square Heroes,' 'Three Boats Down from the Candy,' and the seventeen-minute epic 'Grendel,' which shared certain similarities with the equally long 'Supper's Ready' from *Foxtrot*. (This take of 'Grendel' is also on the 1997 *Script for a Jester's Tear* remaster.)

The session went well, but before any real recording could happen, the contract needed signing. That was accomplished on 8 September in the Manchester Square office of Terry Slater, head of EMI's A&R department. The signing itself went with bland ease. Then the celebratory drinks came out, and not long after, Fish was puking in the bathroom and Steve was snoring through Hugh Stanley-Clarke's very serious speech about the band's future. The size of the contract also drew notice: the local *Aylesbury Plus* gave an estimate of £500,000 for five albums.

Five days later Marillion played a celebratory gig at the Mayfair in Glasgow, introducing the band to EMI reps. The set was recorded and ultimately released as the first disc of the *Early Stages* boxed set. Notably, it includes a version of 'She Chameleon' very different from what wound up on *Fugazi* two years later and the first appearance of a heavily rearranged 'He Knows You Know.'

By 17 September the band was again in the studio, this time at Park Gate in East Sussex. With David Hitchcock back at the helm, their orders were to produce a single as quickly as possible. The A-side would be 'Market Square Heroes,' with 'Three Boats Down from the Candy' as a B-side and 'Grendel' added to the 12" to make it more of an EP at 26 minutes long.

The inclusion of 'Grendel' was something of a compromise position. The song was too long for the upcoming album, and its similarity to Genesis would have thrown red meat to a hungry rock press – but at the same time, it was a fan favourite and an excellent song in its own right. Hitchcock told the band he wasn't interested in doing another 'Supper's Ready,' but as Fish put it, '[W]e said "great" because neither did we!' Indeed it was Hitchcock's dedication to not repeating his seventies work that endeared him to the band. Nevertheless, Marillion's gruelling schedule of eighteen-hour work days began with 'Grendel,' which received the lion's share of Hitchcock's time and effort.

The other hitch at Park Gate was Mick's drumming. He made it through the sessions without any blowups, but as Steve put it later, 'Mick's drumming, which at the best of times needed as much coaching as you could give it, was pretty naff.' The problem would only get worse in December.

The planned two-week session was extended into October, as the actual A- and B-sides had been left for last. The result, perhaps unsurprisingly, is a terrific studio recording of 'Grendel' and disappointing versions of the other two songs. '[I]t turned out to be a big mistake,' said Pete. Agreed Fish, 'Awful!' Intentionally or not, Hitchcock's slightly retrograde sound worked perfectly for the epic, but the two more modern tracks lack the propulsive drive they demand.

September also saw the beginning of one of Marillion's most fateful collaborations, that with artist Mark Wilkinson, who would produce every piece of Marillion art until Fish's departure in 1988. EMI had selected Torchlight, headed by designer Jo Mirowski, to design a package similar to Iron Maiden's, with their striking logotype and undead mascot Eddie. Mirowski and Marillion went back and forth on both logo and art, with EMI in the middle, until finally Fish called Mirowski directly and asked for a logo with a softer feel inspired by Yes. The result was the 'candy bar' logo that adorned every album of the eighties.

Meanwhile, Mirowski had presented Marillion with a packet of art samples from which they chose a favourite, but Mirowski was certain the young airbrush artist Mark Wilkinson was the man for the job. Mirowski called EMI directly and convinced them to use Wilkinson – then simply never told the band that the 'Market Square Heroes' art they adored hadn't actually come from the painter they picked!

The weekend of 2 October found Marillion working feverishly to finish before Park Gate kicked them out, a feat they achieved at eight in the morning of Monday the 4th – at which point Mark hauled himself north to the Aylesbury Register Office for an important three pm assignation: his wedding.

David Hitchcock, meanwhile, moved immediately to Wessex Studios in London for mixing and some final overdubs. With that accomplished he decamped yet again to Trident, then Air Studios, then back to Trident, to master the single. By the time all was done, the producer had been working for 48 hours without a break. He loaded the precious master tapes into his car and set out.

Only a mile from home, Hitchcock's car left the road at 60 miles an hour and crashed into a wall. Miraculously, both Hitchcock and the master tapes survived, and if biographer Mick Wall is to be believed, the producer's 'first words when he recovered consciousness, while firemen still worked furiously to free him from the mangled shards of metal under which he was trapped, were to instruct them to retrieve the tapes which were still lying safe in their box somewhere underneath where the back seat used to be.'

Hitchcock was rushed to a hospital where he stayed through November, while the single was released on 25 October and heavy touring resumed for Marillion the day after. As he recovered, 'Market Square Heroes' rode the charts, thrilling Marillion, driving their biggest live ticket sales yet, and earning a video. On 6 November at the Civic Hall in Guildford, the band mimed along to the track in the afternoon and played a gig in the evening, the audience of which was filmed and cut into the video to create a faux-live effect. Due to conflicting censorship policies for radio and television, a separate vocal take was required for the music video, with Fish singing 'I am your battle priest' instead of 'I am your antichrist.' This 'Battle Priest Version' also appears on the *Script for a Jester's Tear* CD remaster.

'Market Square Heroes' cracked the Top 100 on 20 November at #62 and peaked at #60 the next week. On the back of this success, the promotional tour ended with Marillion's biggest headline show yet: the Venue, a London club that served as a step between the Marquee and the Hammersmith Odeon. An ambitious John Arnison had added the show at the last minute, and advance sales hadn't been strong, so as Marillion's van neared the Venue the manager found himself reassuring a nervous band who were well aware they had to draw at least a thousand people just so the room wouldn't look empty.

Until they saw the line that had formed, stretching from the closed doors of the Venue down to the corner, around it, down the next street and around that corner too. 'I honestly couldn't believe it,' recalled Mark. 'I thought someone must have made a huge mistake and we'd turned up on the wrong night or something – all those people couldn't possibly be queuing there to see us!'

The sold-out show spurred a cascade of glowing reviews in the press, including the first rumblings of a prog-rock revival in the movement that would come to be known as neo-prog. With all they'd achieved, Marillion deserved a break.

'Market Square Heroes'

Personnel:
Fish: vocals
Steve Rothery: guitars
Pete Trewavas: bass
Mark Kelly: keyboards
Mick Pointer: drums
David Hitchcock: production

Mark Freegard: mixing engineer
Release date: 25 October 1982
Highest chart places: 60 (UK)
Running time: 8:52 (7"), 26:07 (12")

'Market Square Heroes' (Dick/Kelly/Minnitt/Pointer/Rothery/ Trewavas)

Marillion's first single opens with a promising crash of guitar and a down-thumping bass. It's a curious song, written as a nakedly commercial singalong single but betrayed by poor choices in arrangement and production. Fish claimed inspiration from an Aylesbury local known as Brick, a 'lefty hero' in Fish's telling, capable of stirring up the pub with his political rants. The lyrics conjure images of fascist rallies, pitchfork-wielding mobs, and a 'hero' who exhorts the masses to follow him solely for his own aggrandizement.

The band settles into a rolling triplet beat, somewhat anaemic thanks to the near absence of any drums other than the kick and snare in the mix, leaving it up to Pete and Mark to lift the song out of tick-tock territory. The metronomic effect isn't helped by Steve playing nothing but leaping octaves on the downbeats.

Suddenly Mick's toms are everywhere as Fish belts his anthemic chorus: 'I'm a market square hero, gathering the storms to troop!' (No accident here that the song title uses the plural 'heroes' while the chorus opts for the singular.) Unfortunately, the shortcomings of Mick's early drumming are on display as the toms fail to swing.

Another verse and chorus pass in the same manner before Mark's massive, if brief, synth solo arrives, heralding a sudden break into a swirling, Celtic guitar riff full of dextrous pull-offs from Steve and shouts from the imaginary crowd. Military toms thunder under a siren-like synth pulse as Fish declares, 'I am your antichrist.' The moment passes back into another chorus that inexplicably lacks the toms of the first two, choosing instead the robotic beat of the verses. The vocal hook repeats over an unexpected new beat that favours the metal of Mick's kit at last, suggesting an interesting syncopation, but fades swiftly away.

'Three Boats Down from the Candy' (Dick/Kelly/Pointer/ Rothery/Trewavas)

'Candy' leaps to life with a threatening minor-key climb on the keys, stacking harmonies on each repetition, over heavy downbeat hits and a stiff pulse from the drums. This fades into a descending series of arpeggios from Steve; over this spooky, soft dynamic Fish recounts a beachside affair. In the hands of any other lyricist, the apparently true tale – the title comes from a summer encounter of Fish's, conducted under a row of anonymous boats with only the nearby *Candy* bearing a name – would come out as a testosterone boast. Fish makes it a horror story: 'Wipe the tears from your eyes, wipe the sweat from your thighs/Don't crawl to me with sentiment, my laughter drowns your cries.'

At the halfway mark the song leaps to life thanks to Mark's staggering gothic riff harmonized by guitar and keys. As the rhythm section stomps and the synths twitter and swoop, Fish promises over and over to remember the girl he's already forgotten, indicting every young man who ever swore the same, himself included.

'Grendel' (Dick/Jelleyman/Kelly/Minnitt/Pointer/Rothery/Trewavas)

Across more than seventeen minutes, the sprawling epic 'Grendel' comprises seven unique sections plus three transitions, none of which repeat. It's a suitably colossal arrangement for Fish's version of the 1971 existentialist novel *Grendel* by John Gardner, itself a retelling of the first section of the Anglo-Saxon epic poem *Beowulf* from the monster's point of view. In Gardner's hands, Grendel is a lonely, misunderstood outsider, aching to communicate and judged for his monstrous size and appearance – no surprise the novel appealed to Fish.

'Grendel' begins with Steve's fingerpicked guitar showing his Whitby folk roots. Fish sets the moody Danish scene upon which the monster will soon arrive. Grendel's awakening is told by the entry of Mick's rolling drums as the 'earth-rim walker seeks his meals,' but only for a moment. A variation of the soft guitar returns as Fish describes the humans who will soon be victims, then Grendel wakes for the second section, a relentless double-time during which 'Grendel leaves his mossy home beneath the stagnant mere' and Steve gets a long guitar solo.

Six and a half minutes in, the tension breaks suddenly into the first transition, the descending chord progression of the double-time rearranged with cut-time drum fills and huge synth pads as Fish chants the 'earth-rim walker' lyrics at the bottom of his range. Then we finally hear a major tonality, a soft E mixolydian progression over a faint martial snare drum and pulsing bass pedal. Grendel wanders, 'an alien in an alien land.'

A colossal church-organ passage from Mark, the best sound on the record, marks another transition, carrying us to the parallel minor featuring a faint tapping on the hi-hat, swooping synth counterpoint, and a bass thump like a heartbeat. Fish describes Grendel's assault on the humans as the dynamic slowly intensifies with fuller synth, more motion in the bass, more involved hat patterns, and an octave jump in the vocal.

The last short transition batters in and out, showing us how Grendel 'cares not for the brave,' then makes way for a flat-picked acoustic guitar under crystalline synth arpeggios and a melodic bassline. Then arrives the section that launched a thousand valid jabs at Marillion as Genesis rip-off artists. The 'Apocalypse in 9/8' movement of Genesis's own super-epic 'Supper's Ready' is lifted almost exactly, the only difference that Marillion chops it down to a 4/4 that would be simple except for its stuttering syncopation, easy enough to count if you're paying attention but hypnotic and disorienting if not. This angular confusion sets the scene for Fish's description of Grendel's doomed final assault, ending with the repetition of 'let the blood flow, let the blood flow' until it slams into the sudden return of the E mixolydian progression from ten minutes earlier. Steve's heroic lead smoothes out into a proper solo in the new key of G minor, sort of a reverse relative from the E, then the song collapses in classical style with a resolution to its final G major.

Marillion's break lasted a week. On 6 December the band took up residence at the recording studio that was the only possible choice to put their debut album to tape: Marquee Studios, upstairs from the club that had become home. But David Hitchcock, who in November had wangled an early release from the hospital, was not in the producer's chair.

EMI and Marillion had both been dissatisfied with Hitchcock's sound on the single, and together took his accident as an opportunity to replace him. Hugh Stanley-Clarke wanted Martin Birch, who'd recently produced big albums for Black Sabbath and Blue Öyster Cult and was at the start of a string of successes with Iron Maiden. Marillion were dubious about Birch and ultimately jumped at the chance to work with Nick Tauber, a producer suggested by their publisher at Charisma who had just made art-rock act Toyah's hit *Anthem* at none other than Marquee Studios.

Marillion spent the weeks before Christmas accustoming themselves to the new studio, drilling the songs chosen for the album, and hastily completing writing on the title track, 'Script for a Jester's Tear,' which only existed in bits and pieces at the start of December. The pressure of making a debut record also proved too much for Fish and Kay, who split up for the first time – a break immortalised in a back-tracked message hidden in 'Script.'

It's a testament to the strength of Marillion's songwriting process in the early eighties that they'd written and refined more than enough material for an LP before signing to a label. Nonetheless, they made quick work of the new song. 'I came up with the music for the "fool escaped from paradise" section relatively quickly,' Mark recalled. 'It's amazing what a bit of pressure will do for the creative juices. The piano and vocal intro came together on the last day of recording which is just as well because if I'd had a bit more time to play with it, I probably would have made it more complicated and ruined the atmosphere.'

Trouble was also brewing with Mick's drumming. Stanley-Clarke told the band flat out he didn't think Mick could cut it, though he'd also suggested replacing Steve, so it's understandable if the band didn't take his opinion too seriously. He then suggested to Nick Tauber, without consulting Marillion first, that Mick's parts might be played by a session drummer. This infuriated the band, who explained in no uncertain terms that they weren't about to replace their founding drummer on the eve of recording their debut. But the truth was that the other members of Marillion were starting to admit Stanley-Clarke had a point. To make matters worse, rumours of the friction had leaked to the press, leading to breathless but baseless reports that various members would soon quit the band.

Marquee Studios was closed the week from Christmas to New Year, but the club stayed open, allowing Marillion to close out their landmark year with three back-to-back sell-outs on their home turf. On 28 December they debuted 'Script for a Jester's Tear' in an arrangement almost identical to what appeared on the album, though as Mark notes, the intro piano didn't exist yet – he plays some cheesy synth strings instead, an excellent candidate for replacement.

29 December saw such a rowdy crowd that Fish was forced to repeatedly order them to take a step backwards so as not to crush those upfront. The 30th, Marillion's last show of the year, was recorded for a possible video release. That never happened, though 'He Knows You Know' and 'Market Square Heroes' eventually appeared along with some backstage footage as bonus tracks on the 2003 DVD release of the *Recital of the Script* live video, and the full concert audio comprises the second and third discs of the *Early Stages* boxed set.

Perhaps it was this recording for posterity that compelled Fish to decry the press rumours of band fragmentation in a lengthy screed against an article in the most recent issue of *Kerrang!* that he claimed had gone 'below the belt' to deliver 'a lot of shit.' Later, during band intros in the night's final encore of 'Margaret,' Fish referred to the man behind him as 'the irreplaceable Mister Mick Pointer on the drum kit.'

Whether Marillion knew it or not, 1983 would prove this epithet false.

1983: I'm Just the Drummer

Marillion might have been forgiven for thinking, at the dawn of 1983, that it would be an easy year. They'd scaled the heights of Aylesbury's music scene and broken into London with astonishing rapidity, scored a plum record deal with a major label, and were now comfortably ensconced on the familiar turf of Marquee Studios seeing their dreams come true in the shape of a debut album. But while in many ways 1983 would lift Marillion from the toil of rock obscurity, in others it would prove to be the most painful and humbling year yet.

January was spent hard at work on *Script for a Jester's Tear*, especially 'He Knows You Know,' which had been chosen as the lead-off single and slated for a 31 January release. The only break was for Marillion's television debut, appearing on BBC 2's *Oxford Road Show* to perform the new single after a hoped-for *Top of the Pops* appearance fell through. Despite the demotion, the guardians of the mainstream couldn't let such a bizarre band pass uncommented: presenter Peter Powell introduced Marillion by mentioning *Script* and adding, 'And from that LP – I *guess* – is this released single.' The band gave a commanding performance nonetheless, with Fish especially in top form as he barked out the lyrics. 'He Knows You Know,' with 'Charting the Single' as B-side, was duly released on the last day of the month.

February continued in the same vein, with Marillion closeted in Marquee Studios with the exception of a couple of warm-up gigs presaging the tour to begin upon the record's release in March. EMI was getting antsy about the album, now over budget and past due; Hugh Stanley-Clarke was detailed to check in on the work at Marquee Studios, but Nick Tauber refused to play him a single note until the record was done.

Meanwhile, Marillion were learning that Tauber had quirks of his own. Though detail-oriented and happy to listen and guide the band as necessary, especially when it came to getting the best performances from Mick, Tauber also tended to flit from idea to idea, leaving half-finished pieces behind him.

To everyone's relief 'He Knows You Know' hit the singles charts on the 12th, breaking straight into the Top 40 at #35. This bought Marillion a bit more time – but raised expectations for the LP. The single slipped to #39 the next week and fell off the chart after two more, but had nonetheless outperformed 'Market Square Heroes.' Further validation arrived when *Sounds* magazine, who had run so hot and cold over the past two years, gave Marillion their first cover story as their readers' choice for Best New Band of 1982.

A last hitch arose at the end of February when Fish proposed the album open with a spoken soliloquy, perhaps something from Shakespeare, to set the mood. Tauber, fearing what he called 'commercial suicide' and underestimating the singer's monomania, suggested Fish write something himself and perhaps they could fit it in – feeling confident that recording would end before Fish delivered.

Fish called Tauber's bluff the next morning when he arrived at the studio with a completed poem in hand. Panicking, Tauber begged the rest of the band to talk some sense into Fish, who relented only when Mark suggested he develop the monologue into a lyric. It appeared on *Fugazi* a year later as 'Incubus.'

When *Script* launched on 14 March, the lead single had already disappeared and the response from the music press was mixed at best. While *Sounds* hailed a 'rare stunning classic of a first album' and *Melody Maker* described how '[e]very song is a mini-drama scripted in the florid language expected by its audience,' *NME* called the record a 'desultory scrapbook of rags from exhausted minds' and *Rock Yearbook* heard 'monumental bilge, a gross, idiot duplication of early seventies poetic bluster and instrumental verbosity.'

Expectations were therefore moderate as Marillion's biggest tour yet kicked off. Gigging began in earnest on the 15th, and the very next day Mick doomed himself at a show in Reading. Mark describes the snafu in gory detail:

We were doing 'Charting the Single,' and Mick turned the beat around somehow, so instead of going bass-drum, bum-bum-thiz, it was sort of thiz-bum-bum. That's what it sounded like against the music, so we're playing, it's only two chords backwards and forwards, and Mick had got it wrong. But instead of trying to sort it out, he just sort of kept his head down and carried on playing, like, 'Nothing to do with me, I'm just the drummer.' But it made it sound really odd and Fish was staying at the front trying to figure out when to sing; he couldn't figure out when to come it cause it all sounded wrong to him, and obviously, it was... So we got to the end of it, and he was furious: 'You made me look like a prick at the front there.' When we came off stage Fish didn't know that it was Mick's fault, but of course, we said, 'Mick was playing it wrong,' so of course he had a go at him about it. And then from that point on, Fish was up for getting rid of him; he just decided, 'He's got to go.'

Then, on 26 March, *Script for a Jester's Tear* appeared on the UK album charts. Marillion were praying for their legion of fans to turn out en masse and secure a Top 40 debut for the record. Instead this old-fashioned, over-earnest *cri de coeur* from a fledgling band stampeded directly to #7.

Script for a Jester's Tear

Personnel:
Fish: vocals
Steve Rothery: guitars
Pete Trewavas: bass
Mark Kelly: keyboards
Mick Pointer: drums, percussion
Additional musicians:
Marquee Club's Parents Association Children's Choir: choir (on 'Forgotten Sons')
Peter Cockburn: newscaster's voice (on 'Forgotten Sons')
Nick Tauber: producer
Simon Hanhart: engineer, mixing engineer
Pete James: sound effects
Release date: 14 March 1983
Highest chart places: 7 (UK)
Running time: 46:59

Marillion's debut is a remarkable, if imperfect, record of a sea change in progressive rock. To be sure, there are odd time signatures, lengthy instrumentals, and inscrutable lyrics in abundance. But the material completely eschews the fantasy trappings of seventies prog in favour of dark, modern subject matter such as drug abuse, class warfare, and the Troubles in Northern Ireland. This is prog that stood to attention when punk arrived and, rather than retreating, adopted the strategies of the enemy.

Nick Tauber's production deserves special mention. *Script for a Jester's Tear* is lush, dark, and deep, wrapping around the listener like the oversized blanket of an alcoholic shivering from the DTs. Simultaneously it avoids nearly every eighties production cliché, sounding fresh even today.

Only a few aspects of *Script* mark it as the work of a novice band. The longer tracks feature a few inelegant transitions between parts. Some tricks get recycled from song to song, such as a quiet-to-loud segue via screamed lyrics, or a soft section reprised later with heavier dynamics. Still, the record is head and shoulders above its peers in the neo-prog movement, well worthy of comparison to the seventies classics that inspired it.

'Script for a Jester's Tear' (Dick/Rothery/Trewavas/Pointer/Kelly)

As the title track, opener, and last song to be written, 'Script for a Jester's Tear' carries a lot of weight. The lyric is Fish's purest statement of loss, lacking the subtlety of songs like 'Kayleigh' that would tap the same thematic vein and veering into melodrama in lines like 'yet another emotional suicide/overdosed on sentiment and pride.' Yet there are moments of glory as well: the unadorned roar of 'too late to say I love you,' the paean to acceptance in the 'fool escaped from paradise' section.

'Script for a Jester's Tear' enters like a torch song, just Fish's far-off keening over Mark's rubato piano. A hint of orchestration appears, then fades. A lone synth returns with a perfect swingset melody for Fish's self-pitying hook, 'I'm losing on the swings/I'm losing on the roundabouts,' a play on the maxim 'What you lose on the swings, you make up for on the roundabouts.' Drums and bass enter in a stuttering 7/8, the tempo accelerates, then high drama arrives in the form of a harmonised guitar lead over which Fish reasserts himself in full voice. A brief double-time underpins Steve's rockiest solo of the album, all bends and tricks, then the vocal returns, then another short, blistering solo.

The scene fades. Fingerpicked guitar and echoing bass jumps introduce a new section bearing a catalogue of the narrator's failures. Fish screeches 'Promised wedding now a wake!' and the tonality brightens, doing everything to suggest E major except actually resolve to the tonic. This final movement sees Fish admit his mistake and vow to 'hold our peace forever when you wear your bridal gown' – which he promptly belies by asking 'Can you still say you love me?' over and over as the song fades away.

'He Knows You Know' (Dick/Rothery/Trewavas/Pointer/Kelly/Minnitt/Jelleyman)

Steve's swirling, choked-off arpeggios rise on a bed of swelling synth pads and a pulsing bass pedal. Drum-and-bass hits break the hypnotic mood, then roll like the spluttering throat of someone trying not to vomit to introduce the first verse.

'He Knows You Know' is Marillion's drug song, their darkest and most punk-influenced track and a masterpiece of prosody. The brutally visceral lyrics, written in a fit of end-of-trip paranoia behind the desk of Fish's job at the Aylesbury unemployment office, are nauseous with recrimination and self-accusation. The second person – 'you've got venom in your stomach/you've got poison in your head/you should have listened to your analyst's questions when you lay on his leather bed' – makes them simultaneously personal and universal.

The song is in an insistent A minor; the only reprieve arrives after the second verse, which fades into an unexpectedly gentle keyboard throbbing in the parallel major. This passes quickly enough, crashing back into a keyboard solo, then a guitar solo. There's more song after the break than before it, driving relentlessly to its final collapse and a little coda featuring Fish calling a secretary at the Marquee Club and yelling at her (for which he later apologised).

'The Web' (Dick/Rothery/Trewavas/Pointer/Kelly/Minnitt/Jelleyman)
'The Web' was Fish's first contribution to Marillion, arriving in something remarkably close to its final form during his initial tryout at the start of 1981. Like the Doug Irvine original, 'Close,' 'The Web' is the song of a broken-hearted lover pining for his ex. But rather than rely on cliché, Fish mines the depths of legend to combine the fantastical with the mundane.

Fish's narrator likens himself to Penelope, the ever-faithful wife of Odysseus from the ancient Greek epic poem *The Odyssey*. During her husband's twenty-year absence, she kept suitors at bay by claiming she couldn't remarry until she'd completed weaving a burial shroud for Odysseus's father – but every night, she would pick apart some of the shroud, so that it would never be complete. In Fish's hands, this legend of marital fidelity becomes the aftermath of a destructive breakup. The narrator of 'The Web' lingers pathetically in his memories, the shroud a symbol of his inability to move on, while the mythical imagery is grounded via the details of squalid bachelorhood.

'The Web' begins with guitar/synth stabs that roll quickly into symphonic blasts of synth over which Fish snarls out his opening lines. This bravado dies swiftly, replaced by a single chiming guitar and the bass thudding like a heartbeat. Fish's signature falsetto makes the long verse plaintive, even pathetic.

The massive synth sweeps back in for a reprise of the intro, then it's back to emptiness for the next verse, Fish nearly whispering as he spirals through self-recrimination. The intro returns again, this time as a keyboard solo over which Fish barks the record's core message – 'even jesters cry' – a symbol that guides him to self-discovery.

'I cannot let my life be ruled by threads,' he sings. Steve's soaring guitar solo offers validation. When Fish declares 'decisions have been made' he's rewarded at last by a major-key tonality totally unlike the rest of the song, almost heroic. 'The flaming shroud,' Fish cries, his narrator burning the funeral shroud that had threatened to bury him. 'Thus ends the web!'

'Garden Party' (Dick/Rothery/Trewavas/Pointer/Kelly/Minnitt/Jelleyman)

This blueblood-tweaking tune is the closest thing to a rock song on *Script*. The lyric came from a period Fish and Diz spent living with the singer's then-girlfriend at Cambridge, where the scruffy, uneducated musicians felt wildly out of place among the affected intellectualism of the wealthy students. (Supposedly the 'garden party' of legend was Fish's first time in face paint, horrifying the other guests and embarrassing his girlfriend.) It contains some of the archest, most recherché Fish-isms ever recorded, which nevertheless sound perfectly natural in context – who else could deliver 'aperitifs consumed en masse' with such tripping delight?

'Garden Party' opens with the twittering of birds and people as Mark's ascending major-key synth line swells playfully into being. The song's characteristic stuttering beat bursts to life from Pete and Mick, overpowering the gentle synth like the opening salvo of a class war. Fish delivers his verses with rolled R's that suggest the narrator might be a peer himself, frowning knowingly at the excesses of his fellows. The choruses are even softer, just chiming guitar and a flutey falsetto vocal. After the second go round the stutter-beat takes over entirely for a swooping synth solo later joined by stinging guitar. Stomping drum hits accompany Fish's recitation of preppie entertainments – 'I'm punting, I'm beagling/I'm wining, reclining/I'm rucking, I'm fucking' – then another short solo introduces the final half-verse and uptempo chorus as the beat simply refuses to smooth out, staying as wooden as when it first appeared, one place at least where the stiffness of Mick's early drumming works perfectly.

'Chelsea Monday' (Dick/Rothery/Trewavas/Pointer/Kelly)

Pete earns his spot in Marillion as 'Chelsea Monday' opens with pulsing bass arpeggios that carry melody, harmony, and groove without ever feeling mechanical. Over this bed the guitar swells and dies as Fish begins a tale of a young woman who has come to London seeking stardom but prefers to spend more time playing at fame than working to achieve it. Despite its viewpoint, the song is semi-autobiographical, and slightly patronizing lyrics

DECADES | Marillion in the 80s

like 'patience, my tinsel angel... one day they'll really love you' take on an aching new resonance when recast as an interior monologue.

A roll of drums heralds the arrival of the full band for a typically mellifluous Rothery solo. Pete carries the melody with a signature singable bassline until it all crashes away into chiming guitar arpeggios and harmonics. The synth and bass raise and lower their heads as Fish delivers a low, full-voiced bridge; then the drums and bass lock together for Fish to throatily recite the protagonist's useless behaviours over a dynamic that longs to burst open.

This again explodes into a guitar lead, more structural than a solo, heralding a reprise of the 'patience' section that lacks the compassion of the first. A murky voiceover delivers our heroine's final fate: a suicide, found floating dead in the Thames with a smile on her face, suggesting that her last act was as much an affectation as the rest of it. The drums relent for Fish to recite the girl's eulogy, which is identical to her introduction with the addition of a whisper: 'she was only dreaming.'

'Forgotten Sons' (Dick/Rothery/Trewavas/Pointer/Kelly/Minnitt/Jelleyman)

'Chelsea Monday' ends suddenly, replaced by the hiss and sweep of a turned radio dial as an imagined listener loses interest in the story of the previous song. He passes through snippets of news and noise – even a bit of 'Market Square Heroes' – to land on the martial triplet thump of 'Forgotten Sons.'

The lyric is a brutal critique of the violence in Northern Ireland, where the British Army had been deployed against Irish nationalists throughout the seventies. Fish recalled of his time in the Aylesbury unemployment office, 'Blokes would come in saying, "I'm only actually signing on for two months because I'm joining the army soon and going on my first training stint... there's nothing else to do, we cannae get a job and it's a job innit?"' In the world of 'Forgotten Sons' these same young men are shipped to fight their countrymen across the Irish Sea and eventually die to bricks and bombs.

The first section describes the experience of a combatant in sharp images. The world outside Northern Ireland – 'not-so-foreign shores' – forgets about the anonymous soldier even as he experiences things that will never leave him. A single guitar takes over, scratching out a noisy funk rhythm. Fish shrieks out words of alienation simultaneous with a proper English newscaster's voice repeating the same – the soldier's parents are

59

watching him on television. The thumping bass of the beginning returns, latched onto the scratch guitar to create a synthesis of parts over which Mark's keyboard wails like a siren. This crashes and ebbs, the bass pulses, then Pete and Mick play stark hits underpinned by martial snare rolls as Fish recites bits of Psalm 23 and the Lord's Prayer peppered with his trademark wordplay to excoriate the British government's failure of duty to its young men.

The song ends where Marillion began: the dramatic D minor chord progression written in 1979 as 'Alice.' Fish memorialises the young men he met in Aylesbury in one of the most trenchant lyrics he's ever penned: 'From the dole queue to the regiment, a profession in a flash/ but remember Monday signings when from door to door you dash/On the news a nation mourns you, unknown soldier count the cost/for a second you'll be famous but labelled posthumous.'

'Charting the Single' (B-side of 'He Knows You Know') (Dick/Rothery/Trewavas/Pointer/Kelly)

Fish's lyric remains unchanged from the Roxon Demo version, but the music is vastly simplified. Like many of Marillion's songs from this era, this arrangement in based around a simple D mixolydian vamp, bouncing between D and C major for the entire song. Mick's rigid beat doesn't change much throughout, relying on the other instruments entering and dropping out to change up the dynamic between verse and chorus.

'Margaret' (B-side of 'Garden Party') (Dick/Kelly/Rothery/Trewavas)

Marillion's barn-burning encore was never recorded in the studio, but then it never warranted the effort. Little more than a long vamp in D, 'Margaret' allowed Marillion to drop in bits of whatever they wanted, from 'Scotland the Brave' and 'The Bonny Banks o' Loch Lomond' to band introductions, long solos, even snippets of other songs like David Bowie's 'The Jean Genie.'

Script only made the Top 10 in that first heady week in March, but it stayed in the Top 20 until the end of April, bounced back into the Top 40 in late June on the back of the 'Garden Party' single, and ultimately clung on in an unbroken chart run until mid-August. (It also popped up a few more times in September and again in early 1984 after the release of the 'Punch and Judy' single.) By any measure, it would exceed the expectations of both EMI and Marillion themselves.

But in April the tour was still rolling. A 7 April show at the Playhouse Theatre in Edinburgh – with Fish's parents in attendance – heralded Marillion's return to Scotland. The show was recorded, with the ebullient encore 'Margaret' ultimately used as the B-side of 'Garden Party.'

The day after the Playhouse gig, Fish and manager John Arnison had their first real fight about Mick Pointer. Fish insisted that the band wanted Mick out, but Arnison was hesitant to axe a man who had both founded the band and whose wife ran the fan club. Meanwhile, despite Fish's protestations, the rest of Marillion weren't as set on dropping Mick as he was: Mark was anxious to keep the line-up stable so Marillion wouldn't fall apart as soon as they'd made it, while Steve was close with Mick thanks to their long haul since 1979 and concerned by Fish's autocratic leanings.

On the 17th and 18th Marillion closed out the tour with its crowning glory: two sold-out nights back to back at the legendary Hammersmith Odeon, courtesy of the same daring and aggressive John Arnison who had pushed them to risk the Venue back in November. The latter show was put to video. The night's version of 'Charting the Single' would appear as a double A-side on the 'Garden Party' 12", and despite Fish messing up 'Garden Party' by singing the third verse twice, it and five other tracks were released on VHS that October as *Recital of the Script*. Two more songs that didn't fit (including a nineteen-minute version of 'Grendel') were tacked on as *The Video EP* in March 1984.

By any measure, that night at the Hammersmith Odeon was a monster success, capping a huge tour in support of a hit album. It was also Mick's final show as a member of Marillion and the last time he would play music until 1995.

Even Mick's closest allies could no longer deny the truth: he wasn't meeting the standard the rest set, and having been given a chance to catch up, he hadn't taken it. 'Mick was a good drummer but not always accurate,' Neil Cockle recalled. 'He sometimes got a bit excited and would come out with the wrong beat or speed up a bit.' (For evidence of the latter, compare the start and end tempos of 'Margaret' from the 1982 Marquee gig on *Early Stages*.) Pete said, 'Fingers were pointing at the rhythm section, but Diz had been a better bassist than Mick was a drummer, and Diz had already been sacked, so it was only a matter of time.' Even Steve was implicated, with John Arnison claiming the guitarist made the final decision.

Mark recalls how Fish gathered the band sans Mick in the dressing room before they went on stage at Hammersmith on the 18th and told them, 'We're going to get rid of him at the end of the tour.' Mark continues, 'So we all went on stage knowing that he was going to get sacked after we'd finished, but we didn't do it 'til the next day.'

The fallout from the firing was intense. Mick fought back – 'Mick thought Fish had joined his band as a singer,' remarked Steve – which gave Fish an opening to unload on the drummer completely. 'It was just unnecessary,' Steve felt, 'he didn't want to sack him, he wanted to destroy him!' Indeed the guitarist was chilled by Fish's cold-bloodedness, which was creating cracks in the band's camaraderie: '[T]here were too many things happening for me to call Fish a friend. I could never really relax with him after all that.'

For Mick, the firing was a brutal shock: 'I was playing Hammersmith Odeon one night and two weeks later I was standing in the dole queue. It took me an incredibly long time to realise how much of an effect it had on me. I had my dream taken away from me, then I watched them go on and achieve more.'

He ended up taking legal action against the band, demanding not to lose his royalty cut as Jelleyman and Minnitt nearly had. Ultimately he received a settlement to the tune of £10,000 for both his musical contributions as well as his creation of the name of the band. With this money in hand, Mick returned to his original career, carpentry, starting a kitchen-design business that would last him until he founded Arena with Clive Nolan of Pendragon in 1995. Even then the sting lingered: Arena's debut album was titled *Songs from the Lion's Cage*, a backhanded reference to Mick's 1979 idea to chop letters from 'Silmarillion' every time the band lost a member. By the time of his own sacking, Mick said, only 'lion' would have remained.

Marillion carried on, beginning the search for a new drummer after a short break to film a video for 'He Knows You Know' at the request of EMI's American counterpart, Capitol Records. They went far beyond the bland faux-live 'Market Square Heroes' clip and produced a visual representation of a nervous breakdown featuring Fish in a straitjacket, Steve in a lab coat, and Mark's newborn daughter Freya.

After a handful of auditions at Nomis Rehearsal Studios, Marillion settled on Andy Ward, the subtle, dextrous drummer of seventies prog heroes Camel, who happened to poke his head into the room and was convinced to take a seat behind the drum kit. 'When we bumped into him it was like manna from heaven,' Steve recalled. Andy fit neatly into the band dynamic when he joined up in early May and debuted a week later at a secret show (as the Skyline Drifters) at the outgrown Marquee.

Aside from an appearance on *Old Grey Whistle Test* performing a somewhat ragged 'Forgotten Sons' and Marillion's first gigs on the European continent via low billing at two German festivals, May was mostly spent working on new material at a rehearsal studio in Monmouth, Wales. The band paused to dress up as naughty schoolboys for the 'Garden Party' video shoot on the 29th, Andy taking Mick's place despite not having appeared on the song.

The single released on 6 June and entered the UK singles chart at #24 on the 18th. It was enough for an invitation, however begrudging, to appear on *Top of the Pops*, which Marillion did on 16 June. There was only one stipulation: as was *TotP* tradition, the band were to mime along to the cut-down single edit of the song rather than actually play any music, offending the hard-working musicians and marking Andy's second time in a month pretending to be Mick on video.

Luckily Fish knew just how to tweak the BBC in return. The single version had already replaced the radio-unfriendly lyric 'I'm rucking, I'm fucking' with 'I'm miming.' When that line came around, the singer shut his mouth, passed a finger over his lips, and waggled his eyebrows knowingly. No wonder none of the other bands wanted to hang with Marillion after the broadcast.

Meanwhile, 'He Knows You Know' was getting American airplay, entering the Billboard Mainstream Rock chart at #21 and hanging on for three more weeks in anticipation of Marillion's first US tour. Back in Wales, songwriting with Andy was proving a grind. By the middle of the month, Marillion had only one new song, 'Assassing,' to debut at festivals in Wales and England. Luckily their debut was still steaming along, as *Script* entered the Billboard 200 in the US and 'Garden Party' climbed to #16 in the UK, giving Marillion their first Top 20 single.

A pair of festivals in Denmark and the Netherlands kicked off July. Andy, who'd slotted into Marillion so well in May, was already beginning to wear on them. In a hard-partying band, his drinking seemed to come from a darker place and led to embarrassing behaviour in inappropriate places, such as dinner with EMI executives or the streets of Harlem. But America, where *Script* had topped out at #175, awaited conquering.

Marillion's inaugural US tour kicked off on 14 July. The band split their nights between headlining Marquee-sized clubs, such as Toad's Place in New Haven, Connecticut, and supporting Todd Rundgren's Utopia at larger venues and festivals. At headline gigs, Marillion played 'He Knows You Know' twice a night, once in the set and once as an encore, with Fish sure to remind the audience it was their debut American single.

For a band who'd conquered the UK with monomaniacal swiftness, America was a lesson in humility. Fish said at tour's end, 'It could well have been dangerous to stay in Britain because any ego problems that we might have developed over there have disappeared... [W]e're having to go out and fight to win an audience.'

Meanwhile, relations with Andy had deteriorated further. The strain of touring led to harder drinking, which in turn made him an unpredictable performer and tourmate. He fought with the rest of the band, whom he considered self-important upstarts, and revealed he'd been forced out of Camel after cutting his wrists in a suicide attempt that damaged his drumming. By the final East Coast show on 8 August Andy's behaviour had grown so erratic – 'a near nervous breakdown,' Fish would call it – that Marillion fired him immediately after the gig, cancelled their planned West Coast dates, and packed the drummer back to England on a 6 am flight the next day.

With less than three weeks before the Reading Festival, Marillion were again drummerless. Hasty auditions were held at Nomis and the band grabbed session pro John Marter, who caught the curse of Brian Jelleyman as he is often referred to as John 'Martyr.' John was a straight ahead rock drummer and never intended to be a permanent member of the band, but he learned quickly, and after a single warm-up at the Royal Court Theatre in Liverpool, hit the stage at Reading on 27 August.

In true Marillion tradition, the band overcame the odds yet again to deliver another standout show. Surprise opener 'Grendel' earned a roar of approval from the crowd; the fledgeling 'Assassing' won those old fans over. The show was recorded and appears as disc four of the *Early Stages* boxed set, giving us a record of John's take on a number of Marillion classics. His rock roots are readily apparent as he bashes his way through an appealingly hard-hitting 'Grendel,' the last time Marillion ever played the song. But the standout is the absolute best version of 'Charting the Single' put to tape, in which Fish's voice trips lightly over a beat that finally has the propulsion it always demanded but Mick never quite supplied.

After the Reading victory, which *Melody Maker* called 'theatrically gripping and musically dynamic,' John was invited back to Marquee Studios to record with Nick Tauber in a sort of belated official tryout. On 8 September Marillion put down new versions of 'Market Square Heroes' and 'Three Boats Down from the Candy,' intending to release them as an American single instead of recycling the original takes from the year before. Capitol ultimately turned the single down, but the tracks would resurface as a double B-side for 'Punch and Judy' in 1984.

Script for a Jester's Tear was certified a silver album, with 60,000 copies sold, the next day. Then it was back to the US for a five-night residency supporting Rush at Radio City Music Hall. The band was already cooling on John, whom they felt lacked the finesse of a proper prog drummer (and was possibly a bit too chatty as well), and the Rush dates sealed the deal. Fans of the Canadian trio – who had edged ever closer to synthy pop with their recent release *Signals* – despised the rough-edged melodrama of this brash opener. The jeering, booing audience response was neatly summarized by a gentleman in the front row who dropped his trousers and mooned the band.

But as happened so often for Marillion, the audience contained an important member: Jonathan Mover, a Boston-born drum prodigy who had played for Toyah and gone to check out Marillion on the recommendation of their bassist. (Supposedly future Dream Theater drummer Mike Portnoy was also at one of these gigs.) Jonathan was invited backstage to meet the band after their final show and accepted their invitation to audition back in England. On 29 September he became Marillion's fourth drummer of the year.

Jonathan's first and only gig with Marillion came two days later at the Baunatal in Germany, a show broadcast live on German radio. Given the circumstances, Jonathan's performance is admirable, but his imperfect fit in the band is readily apparent. The Berklee-schooled player's style is almost overly technical, lacking a certain British subtleness that the band required; he would make a better match with Joe Satriani later in the decade.

After Germany, Marillion decamped to Wales yet again to take another stab at writing the next album. With the tour over and *Script* finally gone from the charts, EMI was hungry for a follow-up. The band got to work, but things were hardly easier than they had been with Andy or John.

As was tradition, it was Fish who first voiced his doubts at maximum volume. At a band dinner, the singer suggested that the new record be a concept album, and Jonathan disagreed in strong terms. Things got heated – Jonathan has since maintained that Fish used anti-Semitic slurs against him during the argument, which the singer denies – and a few days later Fish told Marillion they could keep either their drummer or their singer.

So the young American was turned out in record time, but not before helping to write and demo 'Incubus,' 'Jigsaw,' and 'Punch and Judy,' the last of which he received a songwriting credit for. (The rest of Marillion roll their eyes at this. Fish: 'He receives royalties for his part in the writing of "Punch and Judy" which is based around a Bo Diddley beat which was my initial idea to use. The lyric was written in 1982 with that rhythm in mind. As far as I'm concerned [Jonathan] played the drums!')

During the sessions, *Recital of the Script*, the video of Mick's final show, was released on 10 October. But EMI was panicking. Marillion had only ground out a few songs for a record that needed to live up to their debut, and now they'd lost yet another drummer. John Arnison suggested bringing in a session player simply to get some work done, and the band acquiesced. Top of the list was Ian Mosley, who'd recently done great work with Steve Hackett and had even expressed interest in filling Marillion's drum slot only to find out Jonathan had gotten the gig.

Arnison, cautious after so many disasters, invited Ian out to Monmouth to meet the band without making any promises. The drummer arrived around tea-time on an October afternoon and found Fish alone in the canteen. 'As soon as I walked in,' Ian recalled, 'I saw the glint in his eye and I knew we would get on well. I asked Fish what had happened with Jonathan Mover, he said, "He's American." So I said, "You'll get on well with my [American] wife then." Fish just put his head in his hands.'

The dry attitude brought by Ian – long-faced and sleepy-eyed, driving a cool car, seemingly ancient at 30 years old – made a similar impression on the rest of Marillion. From the very first they knew he was the right man for the throne, but having been burned four times already Marillion cautiously hired him on only as a session man for the writing sessions, which were productive considering they doubled as crash rehearsals. Ian's first gig on the 27th debuted rough versions of 'Emerald Lies,' 'Jigsaw,' 'Incubus,' 'Punch and Judy,' and a rearranged 'She Chameleon.' Added to 'Assassing' these provided the new album with all but one song – as with *Script for a Jester's Tear*, Marillion needed a title track.

Four more gigs followed, culminating in another secret show at the Marquee under the name Lufthansa Airport Terminal, the day before Halloween. After two more weeks in Monmouth, Marillion decamped to Richard Branson's Manor Studios outside Oxford to begin recording. Nick Tauber returned to produce, Simon Hanhart was tapped as sound engineer, while Ian was still just a session player – and this session would be one of his most difficult.

'We went into the studio unprepared, to say the least,' Pete recalled. 'We hadn't even finished the writing.' Meanwhile, The Manor was plagued by technical problems that slowed recording to a crawl and Tauber was suffering from issues of his own. 'He had a bit of a domestic problem,' Ian said. 'He wanted to work on Christmas Day – that's always a bit of a giveaway.'

Tauber's inconstant attention to detail, which the band had tolerated as newbies at Marquee Studios, now proved infuriating. Ian gave an example: 'He was making me change my drum heads every day. Once, he asked me to change them when they'd only been used for half an hour. I left them, went away for a bit, came back and said, "How's that?" Nick agreed it was much better!' Fed up, Marillion decided to drop Tauber and have Hanhart produce, but it was not to be. 'We'd just managed to talk Nick out of finishing the project,' Pete explained, 'when a chap came down from EMI, who wasn't privy to all of this, and he persuaded Nick to carry on.'

On 23 December time ran out at The Manor. EMI had wanted the album done by then, but the finish line was nowhere near, leaving Marillion without a recording studio. John Arnison suggested a short tour to regroup, so Marillion played five shows between Christmas and New Year's, including the Hammersmith Odeon, Friars, and a New Year's eve closer at the Edinburgh Playhouse.

It was during this mini-tour that Ian graduated from session man to full-time member, and he remembers those gigs with pleasure. 'When we walked out on stage I felt something special, I can't put my finger on it, I can't pin it down. Before Marillion, I'd played with some top musicians – you can get four or five fantastic musicians together and they won't always get that same magic.' The rest of Marillion upgraded, too, as Ian refused to work for the band's current wage of 75 pounds a week. 'So we all got a wage rise to 150 quid,' he recalled. 'I was really popular after that!'

At the bitter end of a harrowing year, Marillion were finally back in shape, taking a form that would last until 1988 and see them through their greatest heights. Fish and Kay had even gotten back together, and after some 'bouncing about,' settled in an apartment in ritzy Belsize Park. But before the band could relax, *Fugazi* had to be finished, and there wasn't a studio to do it in.

1984: Passion, Pain and Pride

With the Manor no longer available at the start of 1984, Marillion moved to Maison Rouge Recording Studios in London. Soon they'd worn out their welcome there as well, and the *Fugazi* sessions devolved into a series of late-night taxi rides between studios. Fish began his vocals at Maison Rouge and finished them at Pete Townshend's Eel Pie. During a spell at Trevor Horn's Sarm Studios, the band picked up assistant engineer Dave Meegan, taking him along to break down recording equipment at one studio, bring it to another, and have it set up by morning for recording to start again.

Next came mixing. Fish set off to do promo as Mark and Steve primarily represented the band at the mixing boards of Maison Rouge, Odyssey Recording Studios, Wessex Sound, and ultimately even Abbey Road, where Tony Platt mixed 'Incubus' and 'Fugazi' while Nick Tauber and Simon Hanhart shuttled between Odyssey and Wessex with the other tapes. Fish recounted a bad moment at Odyssey: 'Ten hours or so into the mix the desk computer crashed dumping all the work so far. Nick burst into tears and slumped over the desk and we all looked at each other before trying to reassemble both Nick and the mix before getting into taxis to head to Abbey Road to hear a mix of 'Incubus'.'

The first track finished was 'Punch and Judy', just in time for a 30 January single release. The intended B-side was 'Emerald Lies,' but for either artistic or time-pressure reasons that song was moved to *Fugazi* and replaced with the versions of 'Market Square Heroes' and 'Three Boats Down from the Candy' that John Marter had played on the year before.

Reviews were mixed, though even Marillion's detractors admitted that the band had put out a proper single. *Record Mirror* gave the unkindest cut of all when it reiterated the opinion that Marillion had 'nicked a whole group – Genesis' and described the single as 'Fish stumbl[ing] about yelling "punch punch punch" as if he was Terry Lawless on a Frank Bruno training session.'

February launched a spate of television appearances intended to boost the new song. Marillion taped 'Punch and Judy' for *Top of the Pops* on the 2nd, and 'Punch' plus 'Assassing' for *Oxford Road Show* on the 4th, to which 'Steve and Mark arrived blood eyed from mixing in London only hours before live transmission' per Fish. On the 6th they did 'Assassing' at kids' music show *Razzmatazz*, and if the lyrical content was inappropriate for the sea of bouncing tween boys nobody seemed to mind, least of all

Fish, who appears to be having the time of his life from when the lights go up to the moment he taps a front-row boy on the nose for the final 'my friend' of the tune. Indeed the singer went on to say of *TotP*, 'I didn't know why the hell we did that awful place... We had actually more fun doing *Razzmatazz* than doing *Top of the Pops*. *Razzmatazz* is a brilliant place.'

On the 7th Marillion were back in the studio; concerts the next two days intended to kick off the *Fugazi* tour were rescheduled as the album was still being recorded. On the 11th Marillion left Tauber and Hanhart to finish mixing and hit the road with a sold-out show at Leeds University. Too, 'Punch and Judy' entered the charts that day at its high-water mark of #29, a disappointment after 'Garden Party.'

Mixing on *Fugazi* finally wrapped on 13 February. A copy was sent up to Liverpool, where Marillion were playing that night, so they could rent an hour at Amazon Studios and actually hear the record that had taken so much out of them. As biographer Claus Nygaard has it, 'They were not impressed, obviously feeling they had been out of control.'

18 February encapsulated the see-saw emotions of the period. 'Punch and Judy' slipped to #32, prompting Fish to rave about all the time wasted on lip-synced TV promos. (It would last only two more weeks on the charts.) But the day also saw the results from the *Sounds* annual readers' poll. All of Marillion (save newbie Ian) placed in the top twenty for their instruments, including Mark at #4 and Fish at #7. *Script for a Jester's Tear* earned the #2 record of 1983, behind only Dio's *Holy Diver*. Best of all, Marillion graduated from Best New Band of 1982 to Best Band of 1983.

Fugazi still wasn't ready, but the tour was in full swing and a single had gone out, so *Script* re-entered the charts, where it would flit in and out of the Top 100 for the next five weeks, ultimately selling half as many units as it had upon release and hitting 90,000 in the UK. On the 27th *Fugazi* missed another release deadline and was promised for the next week. Luckily the mismanagement of the record – which the band has mostly blamed on Tauber, with whom they would not work again – did nothing to dampen fans' spirits. The so-called *Fugazi* tour was a sell-out everywhere it went, with extra dates being added as quickly as John Arnison could book them.

5 March came and went with no *Fugazi*, but saw a mobile recording studio arrive at De Montfort Hall in Leicester to capture Marillion's battle-tested live set. Much was made of this recording in the years to come. 'Forgotten Sons' and the new closing double-header of 'Garden Party' and 'Market Square Heroes' appeared on *Real to Reel* later in 1984. 'Fugazi'

and 'Script for a Jester's Tear' were used on the *Brief Encounter* EP in 1986, the same year that an edited version of 'Garden Party' got recycled onto a German 12" called *Welcome to the Garden Party*. In 1988, the farewell-to-Fish live album *The Thieving Magpie* would pull 'Chelsea Monday' from the show.

Of these the standout is 'Market Square Heroes,' played in its definitive version that night in Leicester. All the prog trappings are stripped away, leaving the steel bones of a rock song. Ian and Pete smooth out the bopping beat that Fish often jokingly called 'bouncy-poos' into a rolling gallop; Steve's guitar break eschews precision for teeth and guts.

The next night's show at City Hall in Sheffield was also taped, providing 'He Knows You Know,' 'Jigsaw,' 'Script for a Jester's Tear,' and 'Fugazi' to *The Thieving Magpie*. Then, from the 9th to the 11th, the tour climaxed in three sold-out shows at the Hammersmith Odeon, capping Marillion's most successful run through the UK yet.

All before the album had come out.

Fugazi finally released on 12 March alongside *The Video EP*, a VHS cassette featuring 'Grendel' and 'The Web' from the same show as *Recital of the Script*. (Not only was it four drummers behind, the setlist was dated – Ian has never learned 'Grendel.') The tour ended that night in Chippenham in front of the cameras of BBC 2's *Sight and Sound in Concert*. Marillion don't lack for enthusiasm on the broadcast – as presenter Steve Blacknell announces the band, Fish hooks a massive knife around his throat and sticks a finger in his ear – but the grind of a month on the road is evident, especially in Fish's voice, which is raspy on the low notes and blown out on his signature highs.

The break that ran to the end of April was vital, but as Marillion settled back in Aylesbury for their first freedom in ages, they had to grapple with the reception to *Fugazi*. It had hit silver status with 60,000 records sold in only a few days, but reviews were mixed. *Record Mirror* made an about-face from February and called the album 'full of passion, pain and pride. An album to see stars by.' To *Melody Maker* it was 'more irritating than stimulating, stubbornly clinging to outgrown limits.' *New Musical Express* heard 'prissy and pretentious English art rock – the work of a group who, while paying lip service to some notion of rebellion, cater to and draw from a distinctly middle class/grammar school idea of progressive rock operatics.' And again came the Genesis comparisons, to the extent that Mark commented, 'We're actually throwing out ideas, good ideas at that because we are scared people will think they sound too much like [Genesis].'

The most cutting criticism was saved for Fish's lyrics. Not every reviewer denigrated them, but even the otherwise friendly *Melody Maker* said, 'Fish's lyrics are letting the side down. The songs on 'Fugazi' are piles of images, never using one word where 36 will do.' Fish himself has admitted that there's truth to the accusations. 'The danger,' he explained, 'is that you can become too involved with words that it ends up like masturbation. *Fugazi* became too wordy from an ego point of view.' But the lyrics are also a distillation of Fish's anger and alienation in the hotel rooms of the rock-and-roll grind, so personal that current singer Steve Hogarth has never performed anything from the album. It wasn't easy for Fish to have his soul savaged, and he cut his literary aspirations drastically going forward.

Despite its critical reception, *Fugazi* set another personal best for Marillion when it entered the charts at #5 on 24 March. Success was not to last; the album slipped to #8 the next week, then #18, then left the Top 20 behind. It also lacked the staying power of *Script*, which racked up 31 weeks on the charts compared to *Fugazi*'s twenty. The album had been difficult to write, difficult to record, far behind schedule and far over budget.

EMI wasn't happy.

Fugazi

Personnel:
Fish: vocals, cover concept
Steve Rothery: guitars
Pete Trewavas: bass
Mark Kelly: keyboards
Ian Mosley: drums
Additional musicians:
Linda Pyke: backing vocal (on 'Incubus')
Chris Karen: additional percussion
Nick Tauber: production
Simon Hanhart: recording and mixing
Release date: 12 March 1984
Highest chart places: 5 (UK)
Running time: 45:50

'Fugazi': American army slang coined during the Vietnam War, it describes a chaotic, out-of-control disaster. Purportedly an acronym for 'fucked up, got ambushed, zipped in,' it recalls the earlier army term 'FUBAR' – fucked up beyond all repair. Not a bad name for an album recorded in sophomore desperation across some half a dozen studios, nor one that cost twice as much as Marillion's debut but sold fewer copies.

The fragmented, piecemeal process of *Fugazi*'s creation resulted in an uneven final product, with a weak middle that cries out for more attention in writing and arrangement. Nick Tauber's distracted production lacks the warmth he achieved on *Script for a Jester's Tear*, instead sounding thin, a bit harsh, almost incomplete.

That *Fugazi* is nonetheless a classic is a miracle. Marillion mastered the art of writing long tracks, showing more coherence than the sometimes patchy construction on *Script* – a good thing considering there's only one song under five minutes. Also, Ian's influence is undeniable as he brings to life tracks that would have fallen flat in other hands. *Fugazi* is also a much more modern record than *Script*, moving out from under the shadow of Genesis with fresh sounds and rhythms that continue to incorporate the lessons of punk and heavy metal.

'Assassing' (Dick/Rothery/Kelly/Trewavas)

Fugazi opens with the swirling buzz of a low pedal tone, rolling hand drums, and Middle Eastern-inspired guitar and sitar swells. Fish chants the open vowels of a medieval monk and whispers percussively as the drums pile up and synth stabs climb across a minute and a half of build-up. Finally, the dam bursts and the band falls into a four-on-the-floor dance beat, complete with scratchy funk guitar. Ian has already proven his place in Marillion.

Inspired by a tape of Islamic drum rhythms given to him by Peter Hammill of Van der Graaf Generator, Fish called up images of the Islamic sect who fought via espionage and targeted killings – birthing the word 'assassin' from their Persian name, *Hashashiyan* – for a self-flagellating lyric about his role firing Diz and Mick, ritually slaughtering them 'on the sacrificial altar to success, my friend.'

The second verse continues the ancient-assassin theme with a reference to the Thuggee, an organized gang of highway robbers and killers in India who strangled their victims with a long strip of cloth easily disguised as a headwrap, sash, or scarf. Thus Fish not only hides 'the blade within the voice,' he 'decorates the scarf with the fugi knot' – playing on an alternate spelling of 'Thuggee' to recall the word 'fugazi.'

Finally, the chorus arrives, just Fish keening the punny 'assassing' over

hits from the band, then a guitar solo that plays out the stab of the knife.
A short synth solo leads back into the verse groove, which collapses back
into rolling rhythms for a breakdown, then a brief resolution into a major
tonality, during all of which Fish describes firing his erstwhile friends with
an obscurity that's almost self-defensive.

A third verse allows Fish to indict the rest of Marillion as he accuses
them of relying on him to do the dirty work required for success. 'And
what do you call assassins who accuse assassins anyway, my friend?' This is
not the product of a happy band.

'Punch and Judy' (Dick/Rothery/Kelly/Trewavas/Mover)

If Pete earned his stripes on 'Chelsea Monday,' he's promoted on 'Punch
and Judy,' Fish's bouncy tale of domestic abuse. Based around a punchy
variation of the Bo Diddley beat, the song features a descending bass line
that introduces every stanza of every verse. In the hands of a lesser bassist,
it would cloy, but Pete plays with such feeling that the phrase is a treat
every time it returns.

It's also another early product of the symbiotic relationship between
Pete and Ian that continues to this day. Thumping bass locks with the
kick drum to keep the beat alive and flowing despite its stuttering
construction, a variation of the trick from 'Garden Party' delivered with
much more groove, even when cut down to 7/8 time for the quick,
raucous instrumental sections.

Written to be the single, 'Punch and Judy' is the shortest song on *Fugazi*
by a mile, getting in and out with no fuss and no solos but managing to
fit two and a half verses, two choruses, and the name of the song spat
percussively over and over into less than three and a half minutes. The
lyrics are no less punny than elsewhere on *Fugazi*, but the puns are less
obscure and more pointed. 'Punch and Judy' deserved better from the
singles chart than four weeks and a peak of #29 – perhaps it was too
strange for British radio, but stranger things were hits in 1984.

'Jigsaw' (Dick/Rothery/Kelly/Trewavas)

The most emotionally arresting song on *Fugazi* begins with gentle
fairy-tale keys from Mark. Fish restrains his voice for the opening lyrics,
describing lovers trapped in each other's orbit, unable to separate.
The first few lines use a simple F# major tonality until an E major
recontextualises the opening into mixolydian.

Without warning the chorus crashes in as Fish leaps up an octave to belt out, 'Stand straight! Look me in the eye and say goodbye!' The chords are nearly the same as before, but the new melody and delivery centre the tonality around G# rather than F#. It's a key change without really changing keys, mirroring the lyrical tension between the narrator's need to break free from a failing relationship and his inevitable surrender to getting back together. Things change by staying the same.

The second verse and chorus repeat the same trick; we finally get a real key change for the guitar solo, and it's another slick move. The song jumps suddenly to D minor, a dark and painful tritone interval away from the chorus – but the strong relative major of F is also just a half-step down from the original tonality. It's simultaneously a painful break and a small move backwards. Fish described 'Jigsaw' as 'about the relationship that splits up and forever comes together again getting worse each time.' The music agrees.

Steve's long, yearning solo, presaging classics like 'Sugar Mice' and 'Easter,' fades as Fish returns for a bridge that maintains the same chords for a while, then jumps suddenly to A minor to rekey the original second half of the verse, making this not so much a bridge as a Frankenstein of mismatched pieces, recalling the original shape but not so neatly fitted. For the final chorus, we get another proper key change, leaping up a tritone to C# minor – another musical chimaera made of what came before.

At long last, the fairy-tale keys return for the outro, recycling the latter verse progression one more time in one more new key, back again but different, and this time without the major tonality to soften its introduction. It's just one more mismatched jigsaw piece.

'Emerald Lies' (Dick/Rothery/Kelly/Trewavas/Mosley)

Fugazi tucks its weakest tracks safely in the middle of the record. 'Emerald Lies' was well received at first, earning a spot on the live *Real to Reel*, but was soon dropped from the set with the exception of the intro, which would serve, sped up, as a lead-in to 'Script for a Jester's Tear.' And it's a great intro, featuring thumping bass in a tricky 12/8 meter subdivided into seven and five, then collapsing into more comfortable groups of three for a short guitar solo.

Then it passes, for a long verse from Fish over chiming arpeggios from Steve, a section that could have been cut and pasted from *Script* or earlier. (He even describes himself as 'the harlequin' in 'diamonded costume.') The intro eventually returns and rolls into a bridge featuring a lone galloping bass and some drum rolls. 'Innocence!' barks Fish, and the band fills out the loping 12/8 groove as the main man tosses off perhaps his most arcane lyric: 'To don the robe of Torquemada, resurrect the Inquisition...'

This is a song about infidelity, specifically the paranoia and jealousy that lead to accusations of cheating and the damage they cause, so no wonder Fish would invoke the infamous first Grand Inquisitor of the Spanish Inquisition to depict the torture his narrator inflicts while seeking answers. Still, the song never quite gets going until it crashes into a lush half-time outro where the narrator bemoans the damage he's caused – but by then it's too late, for the relationship and the track.

'She Chameleon' (Dick/Rothery/Kelly/Trewavas)

A rare misstep widely considered the worst of Marillion's eighties output, 'She Chameleon' is three minutes of good ideas crammed into seven minutes. Recycled from a 1982 song that missed the cut for *Script* (and was actually much more dynamic and exciting back then) the track became sluggish and repetitive, lacking the gothic drama that was plainly its goal.

Purportedly a song about groupies ('Who was using who?' Fish would explain), 'She Chameleon' does feature an evocative synth ostinato over a descending bass that could have made a chilling breakdown somewhere else. Instead, it was wasted. Said Mark, 'We rewrote the music, that was when we were writing *Fugazi*. Since we recorded it I never think we played it live. Cause everybody said "it's boring, it's too slow," you know, nobody wanted to do it.'

'Incubus' (Dick/Rothery/Kelly/Trewavas)

'Incubus' began life as Fish's proposed spoken-word intro for *Script for a Jester's Tear*, but is here recast into the dark tale of a porn director who attends the West End premiere of his former lover and star, a woman who's made the leap to legitimate acting. Spying her ex in the crowd, the actress freezes, humiliating herself before the audience.

Named for an ancient form of male demon that paralyzes women in order to rape them, 'Incubus' highlights Fish's skill at melding the specific and the universal. Beyond its sordid tale – something one hopes nobody has ever experienced in real life – 'Incubus' evokes the power held over us forever by the people we once trusted with our deepest secrets. It's also remarkably prescient, presaging our current age of revenge porn and hacked nudes, in which a breakup can lead to instant public humiliation, even the destruction of a career.

Musically, 'Incubus' is a mini-epic that moves quickly through disparate sections. It begins with rolling drums and a crude 'oooh-ah' chant from Fish. The beat continues under two verses in the sneering voice of the pornographer, then dies away for a chiming breakdown that evokes the actress's moment of paralysis, the incubus floating above his victim, violating her.

A long scream heralds a return of the rolling beat for another half verse, which fades to silence. A single, soft piano enters. The pornographer steps into the spotlight, taking his solo to croon his twisted version of the breakup, making himself the victim who was 'sentenced to rejection in the morass of anonymity' – a perfect evocation of the abuser's mindset.

A long, liquid guitar solo plays out the melodramatic self-justification, then changes to sharp, stinging harmonies as the narrator starts making threats. By the outro, all crashing chords and snapping syncopation from the snare drum, Fish's sneering delivery has returned in full as the pornographer laughs at his victim's frozen misery. Very faintly we hear a woman's voice for the first time: 'We've played this scene before.'

'Fugazi' (Dick/Rothery/Kelly/Trewavas/Mosley)

As on *Script*, *Fugazi*'s title track is another multi-part epic. Telling the true-life tale of a panic attack on the London Underground on his way to the Marquee Club, Fish repeats the trick of 'Incubus' to make 'Fugazi' simultaneously personal, universal, and prophetic. As in the best of Marillion's work, the music tells the story alongside the words.

The lyrics begin with warped observations of Fish's fellow passengers, the pained first verse sung mostly in falsetto over a lone piano. Chiming guitar and thumping bass underpin the second verse as the panic attack takes hold; then the narrator breaks out of his claustrophobia at the cost of letting paranoia wash over him, 'drowning in the real.'

Freed from the subway car we rise to the streets of London on a driving, almost danceable beat. Here we meet downtrodden immigrants in Islington and the Docklands, then suddenly 'a son of the swastika of '45 parading a peroxide standard,' a sting at the bleach-blond Neo-Nazis of the eighties but just as applicable to the rising white nationalist movement of America and Europe today. 'This is Brixton chess,' Fish explains, a nod to the black-white race riots in that neighbourhood.

The manic stage of the panic attack collapses; only dread remains. Our view expands to the global, reflecting the nuclear fears of the eighties, though images of 'cowering behind curtains and the taped up painted windows' will resonate with any American who bought duct tape and plastic sheeting in fear of radioactive 'dirty bombs' after 11 September 2001. 'Do you realise this world is totally fugazi?' The words summon a martial beat, harmonised guitars stinging in the darkness, Mark's synth fluting like the fife of an 18th-century infantry regiment. 'Where are the prophets?' Fish sings in stacked harmony. 'Where are the visionaries? Where are the poets to breach the dawn of the sentimental mercenary?' As this final chorus repeats, the drums give way to a single heavy snare roll and the song slowly fades away as the band, conscripted into military service, marches off to carry the news.

'Cinderella Search' (B-side of 'Assassing,' Dick/Rothery/Kelly/Trewavas/Mosley)

This terrific non-album track tells the tale of a drunken search for fairy-tale love. It's a classic early Fish lyric, ranging from technical puns like 'decay on the vertical hold with a horizontal aim' to literary and Biblical references. It opens with a slow, wide-open verse groove in G minor, moving to the relative Bb major for an early guitar solo, then again to the relative F mixolydian for a long bridge in which the narrator seems to succeed in his search.

This drops out as a lone piano resets in F# minor, Fish crooning out his self-destructive doubts about the new object of his affections, wondering if she really wants him. A pounding four-on-the-floor shuffle kicks in alongside the narrator's new paranoia: 'Maybe you were always beyond my reach and my heart was playing safe?' This vamp – longer on the 12" edit – continues under another guitar solo as the track fades, unresolved.

On 30 April, follow-up single 'Assassing' released with the B-side 'Cinderella Search,' which Marillion had produced themselves alongside Simon Hanhart. The attendant tour kicked off the next day with an English warm-up gig followed by a week in Denmark, Germany, and France. The band was especially well received in Cologne, where the crowd was screaming for another encore even after the house lights and music came up. Marillion obliged by dusting off 'Margaret.'

On 12 May 'Assassing' hit the charts at #23, already outperforming 'Punch and Judy.' It rose to #22 the next week but slipped from there, disappearing after another three weeks. Meanwhile, Marillion got another break until June, when touring picked up again with a festival in the Netherlands.

During this period, certain voices were whispering in Fish's ear that he should consider a solo career. Among them were Peter Hammill and Pete Mensch, the big-shot manager who'd lost his chance at Marillion. Arrayed against them were Fish himself, who had no desire to abandon the band he'd poured so much into, and John Arnison. The manager kept Marillion working so hard that Fish had no time to assemble a solo record even if he wanted to – a decision the manager would regret by 1988.

Neither *Fugazi* nor either single had charted in America; nevertheless, Canada came out strong for Marillion. Simon Hanhart was brought along for late June's North American tour to capture the new live show on tape. ('I had ten days away, it was great!' he recalled.) 'Assassing,' 'Incubus,' 'Cinderella Search,' and 'Emerald Lies' from Lé Spectrum in Montreal would fill out the upcoming *Real to Reel* with the latest material.

But Fish's return home from the US was surprisingly painful. He and longtime girlfriend Kay, back together since the previous year, were happily settled in Belsize Park – or so Fish thought. But when the singer opened his door upon his return, 'there was only my record collection that was left there... and my record player, and that was it. She'd gone.' The shock of losing Kay hit Fish hard, but there was no time to mourn.

June ended with the kickoff of a two-week swing through the European continent, a mix of indoor headline gigs and outdoor festivals where Marillion were much higher on the bill than the year before. Germany, where all but two of the shows were played, had established itself as a Marillion stronghold. A festival in Milton Keynes – home turf for the band – finished July's gigging; then Marillion were back in Marquee Studios to do overdubs on *Real to Reel*.

Accounts of the punch-in process are muddled by distance. Fish said at the time, 'The actual percentage of retouch was very, very small... I think I touched up five or six words on the entire album.' But others have since disagreed. 'Practically everything was replaced apart from the drums,' recalled Mark, to which co-producer Hanhart agreed and added that Fish sang all the vocals again to let him 'mix and match.'

As *Real to Reel* headed into mixing the Marillion treadmill ran inexorably on. Three months after *Fugazi*'s release it was time to write the next one, only this time Marillion weren't EMI's fresh-faced newbies, nor were they following up a surprise hit. *Fugazi* had sold less than *Script* but cost more to make, a bad position for a band from whom success could be withdrawn at any moment in the form of unexercised album options. Adding heavy tour support bills to the tally, Fish said, 'We were in the red, big time. There were whispers that we could be dropped from the label if we didn't deliver on the next album.'

One mercy was that Marillion weren't dumped drummerless into a studio and ordered to produce, as they had been for *Fugazi*. In Aylesbury for another much-needed break, they spent August and early September working only casually, sharing snippets of songs via phone calls and the occasional pub meeting.

It was a period of stability for most of the band, who enjoyed setting up comfortable new lives in houses their hard work had bought them. Mark had been married for two years and a father for one, while Pete and Steve were both engaged. (Remarkably, both are still married to the same women – as Pete put it, '[I]t's probably more to do with our wives than us.') In one fateful domestic moment, Steve recalled, his fiancée Jo asked how he came up with his musical ideas: 'Picking up a nearby guitar I started improvising what later became the 'Kayleigh' riff whilst explaining that I tried to combine melody and rhythm. I sometimes wonder if we would still have written 'Kayleigh' if she had asked me if there was anything good on the telly instead!'

The odd man out was Fish, not only unmarried but reeling from the destruction of his life with Kay. Grieving and unable to let go of the touring lifestyle, the singer drank and drugged as hard as ever. As he put it, 'the "White Swan" pub became an annexe to my house... and I was faced with long periods of quite empty days and very dark nights.'

On one of those dark nights, an envelope arrived from an ex, containing a tab of acid and the note 'I think you might like this.' Fish took half, then the other half; then he hopped on his bike and headed for Steve's house. The trip hit just as he arrived. The guitarist watched a movie with him, drove him home, and left him to ride out the ensuing ego death on his own.

Having calmed himself somewhat with a warm bath, Fish sat listening to music and staring at American artist Jerry Schurr's 'Padres Bay,' a misty, romantic landscape of watercolour greys. Fish tells the tale:

I was in 'Padres Bay' when suddenly I felt a child standing behind me on the stairs. I knew he was dressed as a soldier and vanished as soon as he entered the corner of my eye. Perhaps it was my muse; perhaps it was the drug. It was enough to propel me into reaming off a large scrawl of prose.

Contained within were the diamonds and structure on which would hang up the entire concept of Misplaced Childhood. I phoned Steve in the morning and read it down the phone. I was really excited although Steve, knowing me well, was cautious and hesitant to fully commit. After all, I had been totally out of my head of the last 10 hours!

August closed out with a last-minute gig at the Nostel Priory outdoor festival where Marillion had supported Jethro Tull two years earlier. This time they headlined. Halfway through September Marillion decamped to Barwell Court, a Victorian mansion southwest of London. John Arnison had arranged a six-week stay at the residential rehearsal studio, during which Marillion were expected to put together the bulk of their next album.

If *Script for a Jester's Tear* was the result of years of jamming, touring, and refining and *Fugazi* had been forged in the high-pressure crucible of the studio, *Misplaced Childhood* was written by a band who knew what they wanted. 'There was none of the mayhem of *Fugazi*,' said Pete. 'We'd got comfortable with the things we liked playing on, and which of each other's ideas would work together.' Moreover, added Mark, Marillion 'were fed up with the whole idea of chasing a hit single and were preparing to turn our backs on commercial success.'

In the writing room of Barwell Court – a former nursery – Marillion began to develop Fish's concept, a deeply personal saga of alienation and the loss of innocence. The first song written was the soon-to-be-megahit 'Kayleigh,' a very slight innovation on the name of Fish's ex, but the band swiftly realised they were making a concept album.

This provided the first hitch in the process, for while Marillion were in agreement on the plan, EMI was sceptical and no producer wanted to touch such a retrograde project. In the singles-focused days of the eighties, the idea of making a concept album (with only two songs, as Fish liked to say, called 'Side One' and 'Side Two') recalled Nick Tauber's concerns of commercial suicide. Explained Fish, 'A whole lot of producers said no because they thought they couldn't make money out of it.'

Nevertheless, Marillion, protected by John Arnison from the worst of EMI's anxiety, had developed a damn-the-torpedoes attitude about the situation. It swiftly paid off as six friction-free weeks at Barwell Court produced almost the entirety of Side A and large chunks of Side B. Fish recalled those days with pleasure: 'There was no tension and the process felt very natural and organic as the curve began to grow and the sections gelled into a seamless piece of music.'

Marillion's warm-up gig at the start of November was a benefit for the family of John Mylett, drummer for fellow Arnison managees Rage, who had died in June of 1983. Side A debuted that night with the exception of 'Lavender' and the 'Blue Angel' section of 'Bitter Suite,' both yet to be written, and some very rough lyrics. Most notable of these was 'Kayleigh,' which would be almost entirely rewritten bit by bit over the course of the tour and only finished under the gun during recording the next year. The original lyrics, while still bittersweet, lack the depth of the final version and focus much more on symbols of longed-for domestic bliss: keeping a garden, mowing the lawn on Sunday.

5 November saw the tour proper kick off with the release of *Real to Reel*, a budget-priced record featuring live takes of songs from Marillion's two studio albums plus the B-side 'Cinderella Search.' The day also carried an inauspicious omen as EMI deleted all Marillion's previous singles from their back catalogue, meaning that further copies of everything from 'Market Square Heroes' to 'Assassing' would never be printed. Nevertheless, the tour, which eschewed America entirely in favour of Marillion's burgeoning continental fanbase, would be their biggest yet.

The UK leg wrapped up on the 10th at Surrey University and two days later Marillion hit Europe. Arnison had cut back the tour budget drastically, forgoing hotels for bunks on the bus with the goal to reach as many new fans as possible, in as many cities as possible. To that end, Marillion had their first gigs in Sweden, Belgium, and Luxembourg, in addition to returning to France and the Netherlands.

Real to Reel hit the charts on 17 November at the very respectable #8. As a live album it lacked staying power, slipping to #12, then #31, and finally disappearing at the end of January the next year. But it swiftly earned silver certification, and more importantly, bought Marillion a bit more breathing room from EMI. (The album would resurface in 1985 with the release of the 'Kayleigh' single and ultimately spend more time on the charts than *Fugazi*.)

Early December saw a long run of gigs in Marillion-loving Germany and on the 13th the band returned home for another triumphant trio of Hammersmith Odeon sell-outs. The middle show was broadcast on BBC's Radio One and appeared as disc five of the *Early Stages* boxed set, featuring the 'Lavender'-less early Side A of *Misplaced Childhood*. Marillion kept touring until the 22nd and closed out the year at the Friars before breaking for Christmas.

When the holidays ended, they knew, the pressure would really be on.

1985: The Heart That We Have Live

In the early days of 1985 Fish wore a shirt that read 'STAY ALIVE IN 85.' After the agony and expense of *Fugazi*, merely staying alive – and in EMI's good graces – seemed a worthy goal.

As January dawned, Marillion moved into Bray Film Studios outside Maidenhead to finish writing the new album and record a demo. As well as hosting rehearsals for legendary acts like The Who and Led Zeppelin, Bray saw the filming of numerous cult films and TV shows, including *The Rocky Horror Picture Show*, *Alien*, and *Doctor Who*.

The fledgeling concept album was still without a producer, but not for much longer. David Munns at EMI suggested Chris Kimsey, famous for his involvement with a string of legendary records such as *Led Zeppelin III*, *Brain Salad Surgery*, and *Frampton Comes Alive!*. Marillion were sceptical at first; said Fish, 'When he came down to see us the first time we were expecting somebody really straight. The guy's done like five Rolling Stones albums and someone like that you expect to be really big time.' But Kimsey quickly won them over via his enthusiasm for making a concept album.

With Kimsey's respectful input, the writing of *Misplaced Childhood* was swiftly completed and a demo finished by mid-February. 'Lavender' had arrived – as Fish recalled, 'The childhood theme also brought up the idea of utilising an old children's song and "Lavender" was an obvious contender as one of the original pop songs of its time.' – and there would be only minor changes from the demo to the final record.

Kimsey suggested they leave the UK behind for the actual recording of the album. Hansa Tonstudio in West Berlin was chosen for a number of reasons that satisfied all parties involved. Appropriate for a Rolling Stones producer, Kimsey was in tax exile, rendering him unable to live and work in the UK for long periods. To EMI's bean counters Hansa was a far cheaper option than anything local. And to Marillion, the studio overlooking the Berlin Wall was the romantic site of such legendary recordings as Iggy Pop's *Lust for Life* and David Bowie's *"Heroes"*.

With native German Thomas Stiehler as engineer-cum-Berlin tour guide, Marillion would soon make legends of their own. They arrived at the start of March and Kimsey quickly established himself in contrast with Nick Tauber's unpredictable and finicky production style. 'I wanted it as accessible as possible, both sonically and in terms of production – everything was recorded as it could be played live,' Kimsey said. Fish added,

We were aware that we've never been able to put the heart that we have live, and the feel and the angst, whatever you want to call it, down on two-inch tape. Every time we've gone into the studio we've always been overly technical because that's what's expected of bands like us. Chris said that he wanted to go for songs on this album; he doesn't want special effects; he doesn't want over-the-top stuff, he wants to hear a song and he wants to feel a song.

Together Kimsey and Marillion reshuffled the pieces of *Misplaced Childhood* into their final positions using a huge wall chart. Recording proper began around the start of April, just before a return home for Easter. Having heard nothing from Marillion in a month, EMI was anxious, recalled Kimsey: 'They wanted us to come back, reorganise and regroup. We were recording the album in sequence, so soon afterwards we sent them 'Kayleigh' and they were alright after that!'

Meanwhile, Marillion, led by Stiehler, were making their mark on West Berlin nightlife. The engineer had escaped from East Berlin under a truck in 1981 and made the most of his hard-won freedom. In his liner notes to the *Misplaced Childhood* CD remaster, Fish offers a jaw-dropping litany of debaucherous tales from the spaces around the sessions. Brothels and escorts, heroin and car crashes, stripping naked in a restaurant that was once a favourite of Hitler's, illicit visits to East Berlin via the subway, 'throwing bricks over the Wall trying to set land mines off.' That Marillion made it out of Berlin alive is a miracle.

Nor was the recording process entirely smooth. Fish's wild behaviour was in part a reaction to the atmosphere of Berlin. He told an interviewer at the end of the process,

We've been here forever... that's what it fucking feels like. We took a couple of days off for Easter and all went home, and for a few days, I was on top of the world again. Then I came back here and depression hits you the second day - bang! Right in the face... If I lived here I'd go crazy, I'd burn. It would kill me, no doubt about that.

In the crucible of a foreign city, fractures opened that would haunt Marillion until Fish's departure. Stiehler recalled an argument about finances: 'Fish came into the control room with a whiskey glass in his hand. He threw it into the wall, and acoustic material came flying off... I thought, *Why do they do it, they're making a really good sound, why argue about money?'* Worse was a fight between Fish and Steve that had roots in the previous year's whisperings of a Fish solo project and directly presaged the band's eventual split. 'Fish and I had been talking to Hugh Stanley-Clarke about solo projects,' Steve recalled.

Hugh really liked my idea and didn't like Fish's... The next thing I know, Fish grabs me and holds me up against the wall, screaming that I'm holding back the best songs for my solo album! I thought That's marvellous. I'd just written the majority of the music for the new album and here's a 6-foot-6 Scot hurling abuse at me! Any friendship that was left in me for Fish went away at that moment. It was like a switch flicked off.

Despite it all, *Misplaced Childhood* was done by early May, on time and, incredibly, under budget. EMI had given Marillion £80,000 and they'd done it for 74 – less even than *Script* and a huge improvement on *Fugazi*, which had been budgeted for £75,000 and wound up costing over twice that. And as Marillion prepared to leave Berlin, the album's lead single premiered. The B-side was an ode to Berlin's escorts called 'Lady Nina,' but it was the A-side, 'Kayleigh,' that was about to change everything.

'Kayleigh' arrived in record stores on 7 May and Marillion returned to Aylesbury to prepare for touring to resume as they waited to hear how their single would fare. The news came with the charts of 18 May: 'Kayleigh' debuted at #15, giving the band their second Top 20 and topping the bar set by 'Garden Party' at #16. It was a terrific start, but Marillion singles thus far had a way of falling instead of rising...

Two days later the band showed up on *Wogan*, an evening talk show on BBC1, dressed like a proper pop group with leather jackets and feathered hair and Fish in pale khakis, black-and-white patterned shirt, and white skinny tie. He looked far older than his just-turned-27, partially thanks to his prematurely thinning hair but mainly because of what else he was missing: the makeup.

The *Wogan* audience went wild as 'Kayleigh' faded away and their prolonged cheers and whistles prompted Fish to glance at the camera with a vulnerable, eyes-down smile that betrayed his gratitude and anxiety in equal measure. The band stepped off the stage and Malcolm Hill, EMI's Head of Promotions, pulled Fish aside. 'That little smile you did at the end,' he said, 'broke every mother's heart in Great Britain.'

Broken hearts break records, and sell them as well, as Marillion learned when the next round of charts showed 'Kayleigh' leaping up eight places to #7. (Fish has also given Hill's post-*Wogan* quote as 'That was brilliant. You just sold another 100,000 singles.') Marillion had their first Top 10 single thanks to the shy smile under the jester's warpaint: 'The *Wogan* show was what did it,' said Fish. 'That lit the touchpaper on the whole thing.'

The next day Marillion hit the road again, setting forth to storm the continent on the back of their hit. Meanwhile, the 'Kayleigh' music video, featuring a German model named Tamara Nowy whom Fish had met in a Berlin bar and would go on to marry, debuted on *Top of the Pops*. 1 June saw Marillion celebrating another broken record: defying tradition, 'Kayleigh' had cut its position in half again, cracking the Top 5 with a #4 spot. (*Real to Reel*, the cheapest and most recent Marillion album, resurfaced on the album charts the same day and earned its silver certification.)

Like the *Real to Reel* tour the previous year, this jaunt through Europe cut costs in favour of playing shows to as many new audiences as possible – including Marillion's only shows in Spain and Portugal, as 'Kayleigh' crept a spot higher on the singles chart to #3.

Misplaced Childhood was slated for release on 10 June but pushed back at the eleventh hour. Meanwhile, Marillion swung home between gigs to mime 'Kayleigh' on *Top of the Pops* on the 13th, Fish dressed in a Malcolm Hill-provided Highland outfit. By the 15th the single had climbed again to its peak at #2; it was only blocked from #1 status by the sudden rise of 'You'll Never Walk Alone,' a charity single benefitting the survivors of the deadly Bradford City stadium fire.

Mark put the band's reaction nicely: 'We never took much notice of singles before. Now we think it's not such a bad thing. At least with 'Kayleigh', it was part of an album that we were completely happy with. It wasn't as if we sacrificed an album just to have a hit single. And I think a lot of people who bought 'Kayleigh' will get a shock when they listen to the rest of the album.'

All those people finally got their chance on 17 June when *Misplaced Childhood* arrived. As Marillion trooped home from Italy two days later, reports were coming in that album sales looked likely to do as 'Kayleigh' had done and exceed all expectations. The prediction was proven true upon the album's arrival in the charts of the 29th – all the way at the top.

Misplaced Childhood

Personnel:

Fish: vocals, cover concept

Steve Rothery: guitars, additional bass guitar

Pete Trewavas: bass guitar
Mark Kelly: keyboards
Ian Mosley: drums, percussion
Chris Kimsey: production and mixing
Thomas Stiehler: recording
Mark Freegard: mixing engineering
Release date: 17 June 1985
Highest chart places: 1 (UK), 47 (US)
Running time: 41:16
All songs written by Dick/Rothery/Kelly/Trewavas/Mosley

Marillion's third album is their Fish-era masterpiece and the flawless
crown jewel of the eighties neo-prog movement. Like the best of
Marillion's songwriting, *Misplaced Childhood* is at once personal and
universal as it explores the loss and recovery of innocence through clear,
evocative symbols of childhood dreams, failed relationships, dead friends,
overindulgence, and ego death.

Also, it marks a deliberate break with Marillion's first phase. The last
rough edges of the mini-epics from *Script* and *Fugazi* have been filed
off, as have the harsh tones of Nick Tauber's production; the sound
Chris Kimsey conjured in Berlin is lush, natural, sensual, itself a pseudo-
silk kimono that envelops the listener. Lyrically, symbols from the first
two records are judged and either discarded (the back cover shows the
chameleon caged and the jester exiting via window) or addressed. *Script*'s
lines 'I never did write that love song/the words just never seemed to
flow' expand into a key motif; the magpie from *Fugazi*'s cover gets his
own song.

'Pseudo Silk Kimono'

Clocking in at only 41 minutes, *Misplaced Childhood* tells a single story
structured like a novel, with an introduction, midpoint turnaround,
moment of loss, and redemptive denouement. It opens with an
invocation, a mystical summoning of spirits shaped from smoke. Mark's
synth walks up the minor scale – a quotation from 'The Web' that instantly
evokes Marillion's grimy bedsit origins – then settles into vast, low pads. A
lone guitar swells in the background, melding with the keys; as is so often
the case, Pete carries a semblance of melody with the bass. The soldier
boy of the cover arrives riding a 'morning mare,' beckoning Fish to travel
back with him, put aside his fear and return to where it all began...

'Kayleigh'

'Like Fish, I have learned to use other people's names as the titles of stories in which the only real character is me,' writes critic Glenn McDonald. 'I make the rest of you up, sailors on the seas of the night, only to expend you as metaphor, and write you back out again.'

'Kayleigh' is one of the most subtle pop songs ever to grace the radio. The music is subdued, almost small, carried mainly by a single delay guitar and a side-sticked snare. The lyric, as McDonald intuited, cuts much deeper than the usual lost-lover tropes. 'Kayleigh' seems at first blush to be a recitation of bittersweet memories intercut with keening apologies, but there's sleight of hand at play. 'By the way,' Fish asks, 'didn't I break your heart?' And later, 'Kayleigh, I'm too scared to pick up the phone/to hear you've found another lover to patch up our broken home.' Kayleigh didn't leave him, he left her – but his problem isn't that he wants her back, it's that he wants her to be more upset about it. It's the statement of a solipsist, the hero of his own story, who can't handle the idea of his ex's life carrying on without him. 'Do you remember?' he asks again and again. Fish isn't reliving their past together so much as prompting Kayleigh to relive it, in hopes of making her feel something.

'Kayleigh' also borrows a trick from 'Jigsaw,' another song about on-again-off-again love, with its clever key changes. The first verse is in B minor, and the chorus makes an easy jump to the parallel major. It's back to B minor for the long guitar solo at the centrepoint of the song, then a brief pass through the chorus progression leads to verse two in an unexpected C# minor. The genius is that the new key is simultaneously a half step lower than the D major it follows and a whole step higher than the first verse. The ambivalence is perfect for a song of uncertainty – the drop feels like falling backwards, yet the raised verse melody forces yearning through Fish's tightened throat. Also, the new key allows the second chorus to maintain its own original singalong key of D, but this time getting there is a jump up, not just a minor-to-major recentering.

And that's it, two verses and two choruses with a guitar solo in the middle. It couldn't be simpler, but the simplicity hides astonishing depth and maturity.

'Lavender'

'Kayleigh' fades as bass and piano enter with a simple D minor arpeggio. The end of 'Kayleigh?' The beginning of 'Lavender?' This brief hint of sorrow is just part of the song called 'Side One.' It resolves to E major for

'Lavender,' little more than a repeated piano figure over whole notes from the bass. We're musically safe: there are no trick key changes here, no fancy chords, just one simple, beautiful progression.

'Lavender' is almost all chorus. There's one verse to start us off, featuring original Fish lyrics that nod to Joni Mitchell's *The Hissing of Summer Lawns*, then the drums pound out an eighth-note build and it's singalong time. The album cut, only two and a half minutes long, features two choruses based on the sweet 19th-century nursery song 'Lavender's Blue,' itself a variation of a folk song that stretches back at least to the 1600s. (The single cut adds a third chorus before the guitar solo and extends the outro with a second solo and some lyrical vamping from Fish.)

With centuries of nostalgic history, 'Lavender's Blue' is an appropriate source for a track that describes 'the little boy's dream about you can walk through the park and bump into the lady of your dreams that you're going to fall instantaneously in love with' per Fish. This was the original childhood fantasy that would be unravelled, misplaced, by the layered complexities of real-life love. It's painfully appealing, but there's a long way to go before we can return there.

'Bitter Suite'

'Bitter Suite' is divided into five sections, the first three named for classic movies, reinforcing McDonald's observation about 'stories in which the only real character is me.'

'Brief Encounter,' taking its title from a 1945 romance about two Brits who fall in love while married to others, begins as the E of 'Lavender' becomes an E minor synth pad over which drums roll and the guitar swoops and swells. We step out of the past and into the darkness as Fish finally gets a soliloquy, which he spends watching a spider – 'Not the regal creature of border caves,' he says, a reference to the Scottish legend of Robert the Bruce drawing inspiration from a spider while in hiding.

Then, as in 'Fugazi,' we zoom out from first person to third for 'Lost Weekend,' named for another 1945 movie. This one concerns an alcoholic writer with a split personality, a pointed reference from Fish, who at the time was an alcoholic writer struggling with the divide between Fish and Derek Dick. The lyrics, sung rather than spoken, sketch a remembered meeting between a train driver and a shy young woman.

The drums finally come to life for a stabbing, soaring guitar solo, then cut back to half time for 'Blue Angel.' Named for a 1930 film in which a schoolteacher is destroyed by his lust for a cabaret dancer, this section sees a return to first-person, telling of a rendezvous with a French prostitute. Tellingly, it's also a return to the progression and countermelody of 'Lavender' a whole step lower, which says everything about our narrator's relationship to love and women. 'I can hear your heart,' the prostitute whispers, for only 200 francs.

A lone piano finishes the 'Lavender' reprise; then a classic Rothery arpeggio drops us from D to D minor for 'Misplaced Rendezvous,' another tale of a brief encounter (taken from Fish's life, when an enchanting woman met in a bar 'never boarded the plane' for the planned follow-up.) Rejected again, the narrator begins to crack, and sets off hitchhiking in the brief, piano-driven 'Windswept Thumb.'

'Heart of Lothian'

It starts to rain on our hitchhiker as the key resolves to a triumphant A major for the first of two sections, 'Wide Boy.' Palm-muted guitar in an easy 7/8 prefigures the chattering delay of 'Childhoods End?,' then the whole band comes in for a few passes before collapsing back into 5/8 as a soaring lead guitar takes over the melody.

A new set of memories describes a youth in the Midlothian region of Scotland, the lyrics peppered with allusions to Edinburgh, most pointedly the 'Heart of Midlothian' mosaic inlaid into the sidewalk of the city's Royal Mile. The scenes described aren't rose-tinted nostalgia – post-World War II tower blocks as 'stalagmites of culture shock,' seedy 'wide boys' out on the pull – but the soaring music says it all. This Midlothian adolescence is a place of sanctuary for the narrator, who has become increasingly difficult to distinguish from Fish himself.

'Wide Boy' collapses into a single lush Asus4 chord from Mark's synth, hanging suspended in a half-resolution until the second section, 'Curtain Call.' Awoken from his memories, Fish lies on a backstage couch after a gig, confronted with a magazine photographer who wants a picture of him looking 'like an actor in a movie shot.' He's out of his body, crooning in the second and third person over swelling synth pads as he asks to be let off the hook: 'the wide boy wants to head for the watering hole...'

'Waterhole (Expresso Bongo)'

Like the plot twist at the centre of a movie, 'Waterhole' kicks off Side B with a hard turn toward darkness. The none-too-subtle subtitle, 'Expresso Bongo,' references a 1959 movie that satirises the music industry with the story of a young singer exploited by his sleazy manager. The lyrics turn the watering hole at which Fish arrives, hoping to recapture some of his youth, into a place of death where 'taxis gather in mock solemnity/funeral hearses court the death of virginity.'

Musically it's by far the darkest song on the album, a roiling pit of thunderous drums, a thudding, unresolving bass line, and a sinuous keyboard melody in a quirky A minor mode known as the 'Hungarian gipsy scale.' The brief choruses vamp on the E dominant; the first returns to A minor, while the second crashes headlong into a hanging D major chord.

'Lords of the Backstage'

A quick rising and falling keyboard line falls another whole step and leads into a new groove in a deep-pocketed 7/4 driven by Ian's snappy grace notes. Fish's opening lines recap 'Kayleigh' brutally: 'a love song with no validity/pretend you never meant that much to me.' This brief song, almost just an interlude, is the narrator's message to Kayleigh, describing the emptiness of his life on the road. The vamp changes at the end of each verse, moving through D and G to suggest a more hopeful C Lydian tonality overall, but there's no real resolution or even a clear chorus, just motion without a goal. 'I just wanted you to be the first one,' Fish declares more than once, but 'bridges are burning.'

'Blind Curve'

Five-parter 'Blind Curve' tackles the challenge of bringing *Misplaced Childhood* out of the darkness and into hope. It begins abruptly, crashing into B minor in a simple, slow 4/4. 'Vocal Under a Bloodlight' briefly recaps the breakup conversation: 'Last night you said I was cold... I just want to be free, I'm happy to be lonely.'

Next comes 'Passing Strangers,' a title loaded with references. It's a jazzy breakup duet that became a Top 20 hit in 1969, a 1980 single from Marillion pals Ultravox, even a groundbreaking X-rated 1974 film about two gay men who meet via a classified ad. Whatever the reference, 'Passing Strangers' returns again to the motif of the love song delayed: 'Still trying to write love songs for passing strangers... all those twinkling lies.' It holds onto the G major of 'Bloodlight,' which becomes the II chord of a dark F# Phrygian mode, and soon the drums kick back up for a searing guitar solo that carries into a new progression for section three, 'Mylo.'

'I remember Toronto when Mylo went down...' On tour in Canada in 1983, Fish got a phone call that drummer John Mylett of Rage had died in a car crash. He tells the heartbreaking story over a Pink Floyd-esque E minor to A major vamp, Steve's guitar chiming with equal parts darkness and hope as Fish is confronted by yet another interviewer's microphone.

The interviewer is driven off by Fish's drinking; the band drops away, leaving Steve to echo alone in an empty room. Then, from miles away, the bass and kick drum beat like a heart over a low synth drone and a faint swelling guitar. Fish delivers another soliloquy, but it's mumbled and indistinct, the voice of a druggie sunken in the depths of his trip, until he cries, 'the childhood, oh please give it back to me!'

The band leaps up for the song's final two-chord vamp, this time a proud A to G with a fluting countermelody from Mark as Fish finally takes notice of the world around him, the dark alleys and gray people of Cold War Berlin. His defiant observations carry through a key change up to D; then Fish declares, 'I can't take any more... How can we justify? They call us civilised!' and at long last, a sign of hope appears like a tattered battle flag in the form of the 'Heart of Lothian' guitar melody.

This ends again in the fat, hazy Asus4 chord that previously marked Fish's awakening from dreams of his youth, only this time he doesn't find a photographer hovering over him, but a proper morning's sunrise after the long acid trip.

'Childhoods End?'

A crisp palm-muted guitar echo pattern breaks like dawn through the fading hangover of Mark's synth. A tasteful drum fill introduces the rhythm section – Pete carrying the melody – then Fish enters, soft and high.

The lyric overflows with hope, from the first sight of a magpie through the window to the realisation that 'the answers to the questions were always in your own eyes.' More tellingly, Fish no longer pines for the lost love on whom he pinned so many hopes. Instead, he takes a healthy view: 'She's got to carry on with her life/and you've got to carry on with yours.'

The choruses leap to life with grand synth stabs buoyed by an almost-funky ride cymbal beat and bouncing bass. The lyrics are even more self-affirming: 'I can do anything/I'm still the child... there is no childhood's end.' When they settle back into each verse, it's a relaxation – the song never hurries, moving through three verse-chorus pairs and a short mid-song guitar solo at a comfortable groove. Things only start to rush at the end, with a climactic 5/8 transition to the final song.

'White Feather'

A rolling, snapping beat underpins a very different echo guitar, fuzzed-out and chiming through open space. 'White Feather' is structured like 'Lavender,' just a single short verse to introduce variations on a grand chorus, and is also built around a single simple progression between A and D.

The personal becomes the political again as Fish expands his self-recognition to the national level. 'I will wear your white feather, I will carry your white flag/I will swear I have no nation, but I'm proud to own my heart.' It's a reversal of the usual 'man against society' trope, with Fish vowing to carry symbols of international peace while also maintaining that he's his own man. In fact, the white feather was a symbol of cowardice in World War I Britain, and of course, the white flag symbolises surrender; both alternate meanings suggest some ambivalence on the part of the narrator.

Nonetheless, as the music builds and swells, Fish places himself at the head of an international movement. 'We don't need no uniforms, we have no disguise/divided we stand, together we rise,' he sings, before a contrapuntal chorus enters chanting for children around the world and the 'I' of the first chorus becomes 'we.'

Mark's synth, buried in the roar of the crowd, flutes out a martial melody as the song fades slowly out to suggest that the chorus will be carried forever. It's a reimagining of the ending of 'Fugazi,' in which the marching-off of the band carried a sinister connotation. This time, they carry the news of liberation.

'Lady Nina' (B-side of 'Kayleigh')

Built around a drum-machine loop of Ian's, 'Lady Nina' begins with a stark kick and snare like midnight footsteps on a deserted city street. A long, slow lead and gently oozing chords introduce the underpinning synths, then Fish's voice enters, double-tracked an octave apart to create an almost spoken feel as he begins the pathetic song of a john in love with his call girl, convinced he knows the real her.

The drums build, layer on layer of rolling toms. The closest thing to a chorus enters, but the song lacks a clear structure. It just rises and falls, adding and subtracting instruments like the ebbing and flowing tide, without any clear repeating sections or lyrics. The dynamic drops back slightly for a guitar solo that itself takes a back seat to the pounding rhythm section, then leaps up again for another pseudo-chorus, then falls off for a bridge and a long rhythmic breakdown that somehow doesn't overstay its welcome.

Huge synth chords and harmonised guitar reassert the changes, then Mark gets a short solo to reintroduce the bridge, this time with the whole band going full throttle. 'You made your mark, just make your marks,' Fish repeats, until the song slams full-tilt into the wall of a snare hit like a gunshot and is over.

'Freaks' (B-side of 'Lavender')

A lament of fame and its attendant loss of privacy, 'Freaks' became a concert favourite that instantly lent its name to Marillion's fanbase, aided by the constant refrain 'all the best freaks are here.' It starts softly: a keyboard ostinato chimes and the drums keep time from far away as Fish sings of alienation in a soft falsetto that carries the first verse and chorus. Then the guitar leaps in and Fish barks out the next set over the thump of kick drum and bass on the two and four.

The beat fills in for a four-on-the-floor as the chords leap up into a bridge, then fall halfway back again for a short guitar interlude and third verse. But the third chorus carries the whole band with it, all pounding away at a rhythm almost like a soccer-stadium stomp-and-clap. This leads to a proper guitar solo, then another chorus, which fades away rather than give an inch in retreat.

Marillion had a #1 record, but their work was never done. EMI wanted a follow-up single ready for the moment 'Kayleigh' faded, so in early July the band headed to Abbey Road Studios to write and record 'Freaks,' the B-side for the upcoming 'Lavender.' Meanwhile, *Misplaced Childhood* rode the charts with two weeks at #2 and another at #8 before slipping out of the Top 10 – for the time being. It was certified both silver and gold, with 100,000 units sold, on 1 July. Even *Fugazi* got a bump, peeking its head out at #100 on the same day and earning its own gold cert alongside one for *Real to Reel* the next week.

On 13 July Fish appeared on the biggest stage of the year, Live Aid at Wembley Stadium. He was moved to tears to be 'part of the awakening of the new world's conscience,' but his sharpest memory of the day was the surge that followed the cue to go on stage, as dozens of Britain's rock royalty dashed to secure spots nearest the TV cameras. August saw a planned run of shows in Tel Aviv, Israel collapse when the promoter went bankrupt after the first gig. The unexpected break bought Marillion time to rehearse prior to their appearance at the Monsters of Rock festival, where they were billed above Bon Jovi, Metallica, Ratt, and Magnum (and below only headliners ZZ Top). Then it was off to Japan for Fish and John Arnison, where the singer did ten long days of promo flogging Marillion's upcoming East Asian debut.

'Kayleigh' had finally left the UK charts, though it was now slowly making its way up the Billboard Mainstream Rock listings in America, where *Misplaced Childhood* had just broken into the Top 200 albums. This meant it was time for 'Lavender,' which released on 27 August.

September opened with Marillion in Dublin, rehearsing for their first-ever Irish gigs meant to launch the UK leg of the Misplaced Tour, which as biographer Claus Nygaard noted was 'soon to prove to be just the perfect title.' Following a gig in Northern Ireland – where 'Forgotten Sons' generated one of the most emotional moments of the year – Fish's voice collapsed entirely. As 'Lavender' made itself known at #23, Fish was told that he had two choices: take a month off or damage his voice permanently.

The entire UK tour was hastily rescheduled as the band made the PR rounds to apologise to their fans. Weeks of shows were lifted wholesale and deposited into January 1986, with original tickets to be honoured. But one date couldn't change: a 10 September appearance at the Marquee for members of fan club The Web. Ian suggested doing a drum clinic, then Pete offered to join in, and ultimately Marillion played a short gig in which Fish delivered the opening lines of 'Script for a Jester's Tear' then stepped back to play the role of conductor as the fans sang the rest of the set for him.

Two days later came another must-keep date, performing 'Lavender' on *Top of the Pops*. Luckily miming was *de rigueur* for the show, and Fish leaned into the act in what has gone down in Marillion history as 'the flip-chart performance.' Afraid that confused British fans would think he'd cancelled a run of live gigs only to go sing on TV, Fish appeared on the BBC with an oversized notepad featuring the lyrics to 'Lavender' handwritten in black marker.

Anyone doubting Fish's charisma, or thinking he could function only as an outsized marionette in greasepaint and garish costume, would have their thinking corrected by this legendary appearance. The mix of twinkling irony and joyous gratitude that had broken hearts on *Wogan* was in full effect as Fish tore off sheet after sheet of lyrics, often eschewing his lip-syncing duties altogether to lead the clapping, singing crowd through the extended single edit of 'Lavender.' He even wrote out a 'guitar solo' card, complete with arrow, for Steve's big moment. The makeup was gone, revealing the man behind to be even more enthralling.

The entire UK tour, including two three-night runs at the Hammersmith

Odeon and an intended live video shoot in Edinburgh, disappeared as Fish laid up and rested his voice. 'Lavender' shot up the charts in the meantime, peaking at #5 on 21 September to give Marillion their second Top 5 hit. Its huge success bounced *Misplaced Childhood* back up to its own #5 slot on the same day; the album would hover in that range for another four weeks before finally bidding the Top 10 farewell.

All that was missing was the tour, so in October it was back on the road for the second European leg, beginning with Marillion's Norwegian debut on the 9th. From there it was Sweden, Denmark, and the Netherlands, where two shows on the 15th and 16th were recorded. 'Chelsea Monday' from the second night would soon be used as the B-side of the 'Heart of Lothian' single, but the first night didn't surface until 2017 as a bonus disc on the massive *Misplaced Childhood* remaster. This Utrecht concert is in the running for the best Marillion show ever put to tape, featuring a smattering of older songs surrounding a complete recitation of *Misplaced Childhood*, vibrant and rich. Highlights include 'The Web,' full of feeling and groove in Ian's hands, and Steve's jaw-dropping layered delay guitar on 'White Feather.'

Marillion finally made their presence known in America in October. *Misplaced Childhood* had skirted the lower range of the Billboard 200 albums chart since August as 'Kayleigh' did well on the specialized Mainstream Rock singles list, but it finally broke the big one, the Billboard Hot 100 chart, at the start of the month. 'Kayleigh' peaked at #74, but the album sold well enough to break the American Top 50 with a #47 placement in November.

Unfortunately, Marillion weren't placed to take advantage of the sudden American interest, as they were hard at work across the Atlantic (and soon, across the Pacific). October rolled into November with the band still on the continent, finishing with a two-week run in Germany that would earn Marillion the crown of Germany's biggest-selling touring act for 1985.

'Heart of Lothian,' the third single from *Misplaced Childhood*, hit stores on 18 November. It tied more tightly into the 'one song per side' flow of the album than the first two cuts and lacked their clear verse-chorus structure, but EMI wanted to keep the train rolling, so 'Lothian' was carved free of its context and edited down to three and a half minutes. Ultimately this combined with the fact that much of Britain had already bought *Misplaced Childhood* to yield a disappointing entry to the charts at #31 at the end of November, a peak of #29 the next week, and a quick slide off the list by the new year.

As the final month of 1985 dawned, it was time to see if Fish's voice-ruining promo work in Japan had been worth it. Marillion played five nights back-to-back, and while the shows were mostly successful – aside from a woman falling asleep during their encore on the first night – they never returned to East Asia.

Marillion flew home on 8 December, just in time for the birth of Mark's second child the next day. It was back to work the next day, at least close to home this time, for another Marquee fan club show to be broadcast on *The Old Grey Whistle Test*. Finally, capping the long year that was 1985, were seven more UK shows that were intended to be a triumphant finale to the Misplaced Tour but ended up as merely the beginning of the rescheduled UK leg.

They were triumphant nonetheless. On the 15th Marillion were the first band to sell out the Brighton Centre; four days later they played their biggest headliner yet to 11,000 fans at the National Exhibition Centre in Birmingham. And so what if they'd expected a break before Christmas? It was time to start all those dates that had been picked up and moved from September. Surely the fans appreciated it, even if Mark's young family didn't. But despite it all, Marillion had done more than stay alive in '85. They stuck to their guns, defied their critics and handlers, and came out with a #1 album, two Top 5 singles, and higher expectations than ever.

Above: Munich, 1984, touring on the back of the new 'Assassing' single. From left to right: Ian Mosley, Mark Kelly, Fish, Steve Rothery, Pete Trewavas. (*Alamy*)

Below: A 1989 promo photo with the new guy: Mark, Pete, Steve, Steve Hogarth, Ian. (*Alamy*)

Left: With EMI in their corner Marillion scored their first *Kerrang!* cover as 'Market Square Heroes' hit shelves.

Right: The shocking cover of 'Market Square Heroes' launched Mark Wilkinson's collaboration with Marillion. The artist still works with Fish regularly. *(EMI)*

Left: Wilkinson's dense cover for *Script for a Jester's Tear* hides countless symbols and homages. *(EMI)*

Right: The lengthy instrumental sections in 'Grendel' gave Fish plenty of time for on-stage dramatics.

Left: By the time *Recital of the Script* was filmed, Mark had an imposing collection of synths. He's playing a Yamaha CS-15, with a PPG Wave and E-mu Emulator stacked below.

Right: Fish liked to don a Sutton Hoo helm and terrorize an audience member for the climax of 'Grendel.'

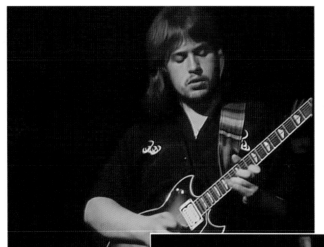

Left: Steve plays an ascending series of blazing pull-off licks in his 'Grendel' solo.

Right: *Recital of the Script* captured founding drummer Mick Pointer's final show with Marillion.

Left: By 1983 Pete had lost his pop look and fit right into the neo-prog scene.

Right: 'Forgotten Sons' on *The Old Grey Whistle Test*, with Andy Ward of Camel on drums. Sadly, Andy wouldn't last.

Left: Andy – seen here to Fish's right – did get to film the 'Garden Party' music video, despite not having played on the record itself.

Right: With his bandmates cast as impish schoolboys, Steve got to play a high-society vicar in 'Garden Party'. He ends up falling in a river.

Right: Marillion's glossy tour programs were an outgrowth of their dedicated fanzine *The Web*. *(The David Watkinson Collection)*

Left: The band's unexpected sellout at The Venue was a testament to manager ,John Arnison's skill *(The David Watkinson Collection)*

Right: With their first LP to promote, Marillion's heavy touring schedule only increased. It's an impressive tour schedule by any standards. *(The David Watkinson Collection)*

Right: Mark Wilkinson's *Fugazi* cover transported the jester and chameleon from bedsit squalor to hotel-room self-destruction. (*EMI*)

Left: 'Punch and Judy,' a showcase for Pete's bass playing, only reached 29 in the UK charts. (*EMI*)

Right: The sinister 'Assassing' topped out at 22 despite a music video that, according to legend, cost more to produce than *Fugazi* itself. (*EMI*)

Left: *Misplaced Childhood* debuted at number one and has remained the standard-bearer for neo-prog ever since. Mark Wilkinson's young neighbor Robert Mead modeled for the art. (*EMI*)

Right: Robert enjoyed fifteen minutes of fame for his appearance in the 'Kayleigh' video – his schoolmates called him 'Megastar Meadie.' (*EMI*)

Left: Wilkinson based the girl on the 'Lavender' single on a photo in a magazine. He looks back on the cover as 'Christmas postcardy.' (*EMI*)

Right: In the 'Heart of Lothian' video, Fish hitchhikes to a gig while the rest of the band is chauffeured there.

Left: Pete and Ian apologize to an angry pub owner for the lateness of their singer in 'Heart of Lothian.'

Right: Steve and Mark in 'Heart of Lothian.' The video recalls Marillion's time spent winning over young crowds in small clubs in 1981 and '82.

Left: Mark Wilkinson was never happy with the cover of *Clutching at Straws*, which was rushed at EMI's insistence. (*EMI*)

Right: The cover shoot for 'Incommunicado,' at the Marquee Club in London, featured members of Marillion's fan club. (*EMI*)

Left: The complex, moody 'Sugar Mice' cover remains one of Mark Wilkinson's favorite pieces for Marillion. (*EMI*)

Right: *Kerrang!* was happy to promote Marillion even without a singer.

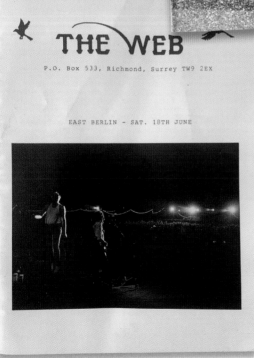

KERRANG!

No 215 November 26, 1988 95p

SO LONG, AND THANKS FOR ALL THE (LYRICS) FISH

MARILLION SPEAK FOR THEMSELVES...

YNGWIE
CINDERELLA
BRITNY FOX
CANDLEMASS
CRIMSON GLORY
KILLER DWARFS
DAVID LEE ROTH
DAN REED NETWORK

NO FISH IN

THE WEB

P.O. Box 533, Richmond, Surrey TW9 2EX

EAST BERLIN - SAT. 18TH JUNE

Left: The summer '88 *Web* was the last before Fish's departure. It celebrated their triumph in East Berlin and looked forward to Fife Aid.

Left: *Seasons End* was the first Marillion release not to use art from Mark Wilkinson. Instead, symbols from the first four LPs are alluded to. (*EMI*)

Right: An edgy wrapper for a glossy song, the 'Hooks in You' single continued Marillion's visual left turn. (*EMI*)

Left: Steve Hogarth reprises his sinister role from the 'Uninvited Guest' video on the cover of the single. (*EMI*)

Right: Marillion play 'Hooks in You' on *Top of the Pops* in 1989. The single reached number 30.

Left: Hogarth on *Top of the Pops*. He provided a very different voice from Fish, but no less stage presence.

Right: Hogarth interviewed on *Rock Steady* in 1990. The 'new boy' slotted easily into the frontman position, charming the press as easily as Fish had.

Left: Mark Wilkinson went with Fish in the split, creating a beautiful, complex cover for the singer's solo debut Vigil in a Wilderness of Mirrors. (*EMI*)

Right: Wilkinson also did Fish's singles, lending continuity to his post-Marillion efforts. (*EMI*)

Left: Fish had tried out the lyric that became 'Big Wedge' with Marillion, but it was canned for being 'anti-American.' (*EMI*)

Right: Fish in an Uncle Sam costume featured heavily in EMI's promo materials, including the 'Big Wedge' video.

Left: Left, a still from Fish's 'State of Mind' video. Right, Fish being interviewed on a bumper car in 1989.

Below: Fish sits for an interview with *Good Morning Britain* in 1990, promoting 'Big Wedge'.

Left: Intended as something of a placeholder between LPs, *Real to Reel* was an excellent document of pre-*Misplaced Childhood* Marillion. (*EMI*)

Right: Released after Fish's departure, *The Thieving Magpie* collected live cuts from across his time with the band. (*EMI*)

Left: *Live from Loreley* features Wilkinson's concert poster, showing Torch from the 'Incommunicado' single above the Freilichtbühne, Loreley's distinctive pavilion. (*EMI*)

1986: The Soporific Demands of Worldwide Acclaim

1986 should have been an easy year.

Marillion had not only stayed alive in '85, they'd catapulted to the top echelons of British stardom with a pair of Top 5 singles and a #1 album. '86 would see them rubbing shoulders with giants like Queen and Rush, taking on America, and earning more in the first half of the year than they had in the entire rest of their career. It all seemed so thrilling, Fish recalled: 'When we started playing those big gigs in the autumn to winter of 1985 it was really exciting. Everything was new: the hotels were better, the buses were bigger.' But success carried an edge. Between the incessant touring, EMI's demand for a follow-up hit, and fractures with John Arnison, *Misplaced Childhood* would become 'the album that made the band and broke the band at the same time.'

The first challenge was the UK tour that had been rescheduled from September to save Fish's voice. This kicked off on 8 January in the traditional fashion with three nights at the Hammersmith Odeon, where Marillion played *Misplaced Childhood* in its entirety as only part of a larger set. All three gigs were recorded; the first night was broadcast on BBC's Radio One and the second night saw heavy use on future live releases. 'Kayleigh' earned a spot on the American EP *Brief Encounter* and the German maxi-single *Welcome to the Garden Party* later in the year. Then, in 1988, the entire *Misplaced Childhood* section resurfaced on the farewell-to-Fish live compilation *The Thieving Magpie*, with 'Kayleigh' as the B-side of the single, a live take of 'Freaks.'

The UK tour rolled on, including a show in Cardiff that was recorded and broadcast in part by *King Biscuit Flower Hour* in America prior to Marillion's arrival across the pond. If cancelling in September had been a near-disaster, victory had been plucked from its jaws in the form of increased demand from Marillion's ravenous UK fanbase, who snatched up tickets as fast as promoters could release them for four additional shows squeezed in at the last minute. Another five nights at the Hammersmith Odeon rounded things out in style, with the final gig on 6 February a fundraiser for Pete Townshend's anti-heroin charity Double O, where seventies prog luminaries Mike Oldfield and Steve Hackett joined Marillion onstage and Yes singer Jon Anderson was in the audience.

As Marillion recovered and readied their next stab at North America, Capitol Records prepared the US-only *Brief Encounter* to drum up interest there. Named for a section of 'Bitter Suite' from *Misplaced Childhood*, the EP featured just one song from that album, a live version of 'Kayleigh.' Live cuts of the title tracks from Marillion's first two albums, plus the excellent B-sides 'Lady Nina' and 'Freaks,' rounded things out. Though it wouldn't sell well in America, *Brief Encounter* quickly became a sought-after item for British fans, who either trolled import shops or purchased copies via *The Web*.

The EP also earned a quirky historical footnote: its liner notes attribute all three live tracks to the Hammersmith Odeon in January, but Fish can be heard saying 'Leicester, good night!' at the end of 'Fugazi.' Mixing issues during the rushed production of the EP prevented the Hammersmith versions of 'Fugazi' and 'Script for a Jester's Tear' from being ready on time, so cuts from the 1984 De Montfort Hall show that lent tracks to *Real to Reel* were used – but the record sleeves had already been printed.

Expectations and anxieties were high as Marillion prepared to yet again attempt the great unbroken market of America. Capitol had only thrown their support behind the tour after *Misplaced Childhood* sold 25,000 copies, but Marillion's American distributor was having troubles of its own: a radio payola scandal that, so Fish claims, put 'Kayleigh' miles behind singles from all the other labels that were doing the same thing but happened not to get caught. Also, Marillion would be supporting Rush yet again, recalling the agonies of 1983 – though also a sign of respect towards the English upstarts by their Canadian heroes.

Despite the pressure, Fish showed a bluff face to a BBC radio interviewer in January:

1986 is popping into America to see what is happening there. I mean it has started to happen there... We have been in America two or three times doing demoralising tours, we have been playing clubs and stuff. And we have taken a very arrogant stand, that we will not go in and try and prove something that we are sure we do not have to prove. If we can get there with the right stage-show, it is going to be easy.

The tour launched with a headlining gig in Utica, New York on 26 February. The first Rush support gig was the next night in Buffalo, where Marillion played side one of *Misplaced Childhood* plus 'Incubus' and 'Fugazi.' Afterwards, however, they would simply play all of *Misplaced Childhood* whenever opening for Rush. A few reasons were given for this decision. 'We decided we should really show where we are at the moment,' said Fish. Pete noted that 'we were thinking of splitting up bits and pieces, but it was pointless doing that because people may as well hear the whole thing.' Steve added, 'Because it does work quite well as a continuous piece of music. As a support group, you can get to the point where you're struggling to hold the audiences' attention, but it has worked so far.'

On 10 March Marillion hit the west coast for the first time with six gigs in a week, moving south from Vancouver, British Columbia, through Seattle and Portland to San Francisco and LA. (The first of two LA shows at the Roxy is the scene for Mick Wall's name-dropping opening to his 1987 band bio *Market Square Heroes*. Apparently, David Coverdale and Bob Seger were spotted singing along to 'Kayleigh!') From there it was the American Midwest, from Indianapolis to Cincinnati with a stop in Milwaukee where a phone call from Fish to his girlfriend Tamara would soon inspire a lyric called 'Sugar Mice.' The only sour note came in Detroit, where impatient Rush fans began throwing coins at Marillion, prompting a lengthy, profanity-laden rant from Fish.

On the back of the tour *Brief Encounter,* released in March, broke into the American charts on the 22nd, climbing to a peak of #67 in mid-April. This was bolstered by a brief appearance by 'Lady Nina' on the Billboard Mainstream Rock chart, which topped out at #30 at the same time. Capitol Records had loved the song ever since it came out of the *Misplaced Childhood* sessions, going so far as to demand that Marillion include it on the album, which they wisely refused to do. Nonetheless it was finally an A-side, though its performance no doubt disappointed.

31 March began the east coast leg of the tour – only four gigs, but all opening for Rush at huge American stadiums like the Meadowlands and Nassau Coliseum. Then it was back to England for a few weeks' break as Blue Öyster Cult took over support duties. The American run ended with a brief return to southern California at the end of April, including a twenty-minute set at a huge outdoor festival in LA and two more sold-out headlines there.

The tickets had sold, and Marillion's hard work had kept *Misplaced Childhood* alive near the bottom end of the Billboard 200 albums chart, but it was gone before April was over. *Brief Encounter* hung on until the end of May, creeping lower and lower as the weeks went on.

Meanwhile the EMI grindstone kept turning. Home at last with their touring duties fulfilled, Marillion were now on the hook for yet another album. There was no question of being dropped from the label, as there had been after the costly near-disaster of *Fugazi*, but the pressure to deliver a second #1 record was perhaps even worse.

Hoping to recapture the easy magic of the *Misplaced Childhood* sessions, Marillion decamped to Barwell Court for the month of May. The session was an abject failure, as Fish later wrote: 'The first writing sessions are pretty much lost in the haze and I don't remember anything about Barwell Court apart from some wild nights.'

There was no time for reflection as the European festival season was nigh. Following production rehearsals in Poland and a pair of Swedish gigs, Marillion played perhaps their highest-profile gig yet, as they took the stage at the Vincennes Hippodrome on the outskirts of Paris in support of Queen. The reaction from a normally sceptical music press was almost rapturous. Nick Gibson wrote in *Music Week*,

> After seven years and four top 30 albums, Marillion are in danger of becoming a world-class attraction... [T]he crowd's response during Marillion's 70-minute set suggested the amiable five-piece could well have topped the bill over headliners Queen, with vocalist Fish earning the affection of the audience early on with his imposing but unforced delivery. ... Marillion, already successful, are going to get much bigger. How they overcome the soporific demands of worldwide acclaim remains to be seen, but at present, there's no-one else like them.

Gibson's throwaway line about the 'demands of worldwide acclaim' may have been more prescient than he knew. Touring life always took a toll, especially on Fish, but gigging with Queen brought a new scale to the proceedings. As the singer recalled, the association 'not only retarded my rehabilitation but the close contact with Freddie and the boys even taught me some new methods of debauchery.'

A pair of German headlines followed, then Marillion's first-ever gig in Austria, where they pulled out a few old songs like 'Chelsea Monday' and 'He Knows You Know' as a gift for their Viennese fans. Next up was a show at Ahoy Sportpaleis in Rotterdam that both Ian and Pete would recall as a particular favourite – Ian had seen David Bowie there a decade earlier and always wanted to play the venue.

Then it was back to Germany and Queen for Marillion's biggest crowd yet, some 90,000 people at a festival in Mannheim. The two acts had warmed to each other and Queen guitarist Brian May joined Marillion's

encore to insert 'Let's Twist Again' into 'Market Square Heroes.' Fish
returned the favour halfway through Queen's set by singing 'Tutti Frutti'
with Freddie Mercury. This show also provided the single 'Freaks' to the
1988 live album *The Thieving Magpie*.

After another German festival with Queen, Marillion returned home
for a festival of their own. On 28 June the Milton Keynes Bowl, located
smack in the band's stomping grounds, was the site of the so-called
Garden Party at Milton Keynes that would go down in Marillion legend.
The band invited Gary Moore, who had held third billing below Queen,
and Jethro Tull, who'd given them their own festival debut back in 1982,
plus Magnum and Mama's Boys. But it was Marillion's night, and in front
of some 35,000 fans – the biggest crowd yet assembled for a Marillion
headline – they played a long set that drew from their back catalogue to
support the entirety of *Misplaced Childhood* in the middle.

Biographer Claus Nygaard points out that in the midst of a perceived
slump in live music ticket sales, Marillion's ability to fill the Milton
Keynes Bowl was a sign of their star status. He quotes the director of
Concorde Management and Promotions at the time: 'I think the problem
is that last year everybody was really spoilt with the Live Aid event and
Springsteen's concerts, and now some people don't want to go to a gig
unless it's by a megastar. Acts like Phil Collins, Marillion and Dire Straits
are guaranteed to sell-out, it's the bands further down in the pecking
order who have the problems.'

But again, the outward triumph wasn't so simple within Marillion. Fish
later recalled that while 'there was tremendous celebration in the fan base
because it was Milton Keynes,' the Garden Party 'was a daunting gig. By
that point we were all getting a bit fried – the magic in some instances was
wearing a little bit thin.' It was a mercy, then, that July brought a break.

The question of Fish going solo was back again, aggravated by his growing
frustration with the distribution of pay in Marillion. As the face of the band,
not only was he responsible for the lion's share of promotion, but Fish had
begun to feel that his dual role as frontman and lyricist warranted a bigger
slice of the pie than his bandmates. Accordingly, July saw Fish record the
only single he's ever released outside of Marillion and his solo career: an
upbeat pop tune called 'Shortcut to Somewhere,' co-written with Genesis
keyboardist Tony Banks for the Kevin Bacon vehicle *Quicksilver*.

Three more festivals rounded out July, including the final show with
Queen and a charity gig in St. Helens, near Liverpool, called Soap Aid.
Breaking from Marillion's tradition of outdoor victories, Soap Aid was no

less than a disaster – 'I still wake up sweating!' said Fish of the gig. Not only did Soap Aid lose money, a fight between rival rugby fans of Wigan and St. Helens broke out during 'Garden Party,' forcing Fish to stop the song so he could defuse the crowd.

On 1 August Steve finally married his girlfriend Jo, with all of Marillion in attendance. As the pair winged off to St. Lucia for a honeymoon the rest of the band got another break before writing on the new album resumed in earnest. Ian and Pete took the opportunity to play on a track with Steve Hackett of Genesis, but Fish recalls this as one of the most difficult periods in his time with Marillion. He was coming out of his stretch of heaviest drug abuse, kicked off in 1985 by the pressures of success and prolonged by the heady summer of 1986. He later wrote of that time,

> That entire era was a blur of travelling, performing and endless interviews combined with the excesses of a touring rock band with their first worldwide hit. I was wasted physically and spiritually at the end of that road. The band had been well tested on the recent tour in every conceivable way. Relationships had been strained to the limit as we all tried to escape the surrealism of touring in our individual ways and find some private space to hide in. I didn't deal with it at all well and the availability of all manner of temptations proved too much for a hedonistic soul like my own.

Yet the end of the tour brought no relief: '[A]s the dates dwindled to a stop the realisation that we had to write and record a follow up crept in and the white panic of responsibility clawed away inside my stomach.'

Adding to the misery were issues with John Arnison's management, which were badly exacerbated over the last twelve months by the new scale of Marillion's finances. Due to his compensation structure, the more Marillion toured, the more money Arnison made – or as Fish put it, he was 'living a lifestyle that was reliant on the band being out on tour.' Pete was a little more forgiving, but only a little: 'I don't think John set out to rip us off, but touring was a way for him to make money.' In addition, Arnison's aggressive management style meant that Marillion were perpetually in debt to EMI for album advances, tour support, music video shoots, and all the other attendant costs of a major rock act. The band was trapped in a vicious cycle, forced again and again to return to the reliable well of ticket sales to pay back the latest round of advances.

The financial reliance on touring fed Fish's growing sense of being trapped. Marillion's demanding schedule left no time for the long-considered solo album. Seeking new outlets, he'd attempted a novel and took on a theatrical agent to break into acting, but even that was sacrificed at the altar of the gig when Fish had to turn down a role in *Highlander* due to tour obligations in the second half of 1985. (Marillion had even been asked to do the soundtrack, but declined for the same reason, something Steve regrets to this day: 'As always in those sorts of cases you don't get offered it again.' The mantle was famously passed to Queen.)

So when Steve returned, August rolled into September, and work resumed, Marillion were not a happy band. The contract with EMI demanded an album by 1987, and the plan was to knock it out over the fall and have it in stores before the obligatory Christmas shows at year's end. This would not happen.

In late September 'Shortcut to Somewhere,' Fish's single with Tony Banks, came and went with a #75 peak in mid-October. The fact that the film Kevin Bacon later called 'the absolute lowest point of my career' never earned a UK release certainly didn't help. Fortunately, back in the Marillion camp a few writing sessions at Steve's place during the summer breaks had produced some usable material, embryonic versions of 'Hotel Hobbies' and 'Warm Wet Circles.' Over the course of the autumn Marillion tried Nomis, then Bray Studios, where they produced a few demos including 'a brilliant version of 'Sugar Mice' recorded on 2 track which at one point during the proper recording we seriously considered using on the album,' per Fish.

Eventually, they settled in at Stanbridge Farm, just off the A23 in West Sussex, but it quickly became a place of conflict. Fish found the damp, sagging old farm 'hellish,' which is about what the rest of the band thought of the singer's behaviour. He demanded increased compensation befitting his position as sole lyricist, but those lyrics were losing their value. Chris Kimsey, brought back as producer, felt Fish was 'lyrically losing the plot.' John Arnison agreed and earned 'a huge sigh of relief' from Marillion as the first person to say so to Fish's face.

Nor was the music thrilling Kimsey, Arnison, or Hugh Stanley-Clarke of EMI. It was too similar to *Misplaced Childhood*, they felt, a damning indictment from an A&R man who would surely have been put off even more by anything too different. Fish was quick to leap into the breach:

[Chris Kimsey] arrived with Hugh Stanley Clarke to hear the new material one night and we duly sat back and played him the meagre scraps of the sessions so far. They were unimpressed until I suggested we play him the jam piece we reserved for playing when we came back pissed from the pub. Most of the others hated it as they felt it was too like the Who (which it was) and the opening lyrics ripped off the Stones 'Sympathy for the Devil' (which they didn't). Grudgingly we played it live. Chris loved it and Hugh nominated it as a potential single. That was 'Incommunicado.'

The battle lines were drawn, Fish against the rest, but the singer felt Arnison had taken the band's side in addition to an oversized cut of the profits. After a night out drinking with the manager, whose own substance abuse issues were growing, Fish lay awake 'staring at the ceiling unable to sleep and considering my options. I wanted to go. I wanted a life. I was so tired of the touring and felt trapped by the machine we'd created. It was 'That Time of the Night', a lyric that still reads like my resignation statement.' The plan had been to eschew a concept album so as not to retread *Misplaced Childhood*, but despite Marillion's best intentions, a concept was crystallising anyway: the collapse of the band.

Writing and demoing limped along until Christmas Eve, when Marillion earned a brief respite in the form of five fan-club shows close to home. At the first of them, a charity gig at the Aylesbury Friars, Fish wore face paint for the first time all year to the delight of the audience. But the greasepaint mask failed to return him to earlier, easier days. 'It was completely wrong!' Fish recalled. 'It was like trying to squeeze into your school uniform.'

'He Knows You Know' and 'Margaret' also returned for these shows, and the fans received the new with as much pleasure as the old as Marillion debuted in-the-works versions of 'Warm Wet Circles,' 'White Russian,' and 'Incommunicado.' All three received rave reviews in the next issue of *The Web*, with one writer presciently demanding the last for a single. Anticipation was high for the new album, and if Marillion's fans were ignorant of the fractures within the band, it was a forgivable ignorance, even if it only increased the pressure on Marillion not to fall apart in 1987.

1987: What Am I Doing Wrong?

Ready or not, it was time to make a record.

At the end of January Marillion and Chris Kimsey settled in at Westside Studios in London to piece together *Clutching at Straws*. Kimsey had settled his tax issues and EMI had opened their wallets to the tune of £135,000, so there was no need to return to West Berlin – but staying close to home ended up a poor choice. 'After Berlin, working in London was a real downer,' Kimsey recalled. 'I said at the time it was a mistake.'

Westside was a hotbed of debauchery. '[A] more dangerous venue could not have been found,' Fish recalled, 'minutes from the West End and Hammersmith Odeon, a taxi ride from home and discreetly tucked away in the back streets. We took full advantage and the sessions were intense and riddled with outrageous over the top consumption of substances and 120 mile an hour table tennis games.' Ian described an awkward visit by EMI A&R head David Munns: 'Everyone was completely out of it... John Arnison was crashing around in the vocal booth. David drove back with me – he was so worried he filled his car up with diesel.' Fish also recalled 'Arnison totally off his head talking to himself and giggling insanely as we all sat in the control room listening to him on an open mike, laughing nervously at the man in charge of our careers.'

Yet the sessions were as artistically productive as they were emotionally destructive – as Fish recalled, 'I hated the atmosphere, but the end result was justifying the friction.' 'Going Under,' the B-side of the 'Incommunicado' single, was improvised by Steve and Fish with the tapes rolling. Its lyric of self-disintegration apparently led Tamara, then Fish's fiancée, to ask 'What am I doing wrong?' when she heard it.

The band was fighting, too. One legendary blow-up featured Fish screaming at Steve and ultimately throwing a whiskey tumbler at his head, after which Steve stormed out, intending to quit. 'I'd had enough of the egos and temper tantrums,' he recalled. 'The thing I'd wanted to do more than anything else in my life had become something I hated. As far as I was concerned, that was it – I'd left the band.' Ian talked him off the ledge, but the crack that had opened between Fish and Steve in Berlin was now a canyon: 'Fish hadn't realised how much he'd upset me. I'd made the decision that he'd never get to me in that way again.'

With the pressure on from EMI and tour dates booked, Marillion soldiered on, and by early April had moved to Advision Studios for overdubs and mixing. They were also prepping 'Incommunicado' for a major single push, so in the early-morning haze of 9 April Fish, Ian, Arnison, and long-time cover artist Mark Wilkinson arrived outside the Marquee Club to line up a gaggle of fan-club members for the cover photo. After Mark's birthday party that night, Marillion returned to Advision for the second great *Clutching at Straws* fight. Advision engineer David Jacobs was unpopular with the band and Steve remarked that his mixes sounded 'boring and sterile' compared to the monitor mixes back at Westside. Kimsey took this as a shot at himself and snapped back that Steve was being lazy about his playing. Steve's response was to strap on his guitar, fire up his amp, and lay down the solo of 'Sugar Mice' in a single take.

Assistant engineer Avril Mackintosh recalled this as an argument-ender – 'He played this blinding solo. That shut everyone up.' – but that night, Pete crashed his car driving home. At the emergency band meeting at Fish's house the next day, the singer wrote, 'Ian and I stared at each other over a coffee and a smoke, firmly believing that the band was over. It was the closest we had ever come to a split. Needs must and soon we were all back in the studio arguing over grace notes and vocal lines.'

At last, Marillion completed the album that Fish would describe as 'very honest, very open, to the point where you go, "Fucking hell..."' and of which Steve would say, 'It's a very powerful album in that it's got some of our best work. But you can also see the fracture lines.' The 'Incommunicado' single was released on 11 May as Marillion ran the promotional gauntlet in Britain and Europe, and by the 17th they were back in London to mime 'Incommunicado' for *Top of the Pops*. Six days later the single entered the charts at #6, where it would hang on for the next week before slipping out of the Top 10 and off the chart by mid-July. Not a bad showing, but 'Incommunicado' didn't live up to the cuts from *Misplaced Childhood*. The singles yet to come would do even worse.

Promotion continued through June until production rehearsals began in Poland on the 19th. The preparations saw a number of shakeups. The band considered bringing 'Grendel' back to the set, going so far as to try it with Ian for the first time, but as Fish described, 'It just didn't work - the feel was all wrong, the musicianship had increased and it was actually regressive for us to go back and play the piece.' The tour also featured Marillion's first outside hire, as American singer Cori Josias was brought on to handle the high range that was starting to blow out Fish's voice.

Another development was that Fish had made up his mind: it was time to go. 'He came to see me at the beginning of the tour and said he was definitely leaving at the end of it,' John Arnison recalled. 'I kept quiet with the others but asked him not to leave. I said, "It's been a roller coaster for five years, go and do a solo album."' Fish's reaction was disbelief: 'Solo project?' he scoffed later. 'When was that supposed to happen?' Not only was he keeping Marillion booked solid, Arnison's behaviour was spiralling, impairing his ability to hold the band together. 'If he had been stronger at the time, then Fish could have done his solo project,' Ian recalled.

Under this cloud the tour launched on 22 June with Marillion's first show in Poland, celebrating the release that day of *Clutching at Straws*. With UK preorders in the range of 150,000, the album was certified both silver and gold only three days later – yet somehow it came up short. *Clutching* hit the album chart at #2 on 4 July, dropped to #7 the next week, and hovered around #20 until mid-August. Ultimately it only spent fifteen weeks on the charts, compared to *Misplaced Childhood*'s 42. In America the album only flirted with success, kissing #103 on the Billboard 200 halfway through August but never breaking into double digits; meanwhile, 'Incommunicado' couldn't crack the Top 20 of Mainstream Rock singles and never came close to the Hot 100.

Clutching at Straws

Personnel:
Fish: vocals
Steve Rothery: guitars
Pete Trewavas: bass
Mark Kelly: keyboards
Ian Mosley: drums
Additional musicians:
Tessa Niles: backing vocals (on 'That Time of the Night' and 'The Last Straw')
Christopher 'Robbin' Kimsey: backing vocals (on 'Incommunicado')
John Cavanagh: 'Dr. Finlay' voice on 'Torch Song'
Chris Kimsey: production
Release date: 22 June 1987
Highest chart places: 2 (UK)
Running time: 49:33 (LP), 52:21 (CD)
All songs written by Dick/Rothery/Kelly/Trewavas/Mosley

Marillion's fourth and final album with Fish is a close second for their best – indeed it remains the singer's favourite work with the band. For the most part, *Clutching at Straws* is the equal of *Misplaced Childhood*, a darker, more mature cousin that packs as much emotional punch, but the fractures within Marillion are visible.

Clutching at Straws is a concept album that can't quite commit. In a 1989 interview heralding the release of *Seasons End*, Mark was asked why Marillion had moved away from concept albums. His response: 'The only real concept album we did was *Misplaced Childhood*... [*Clutching at Straws*] is a personal statement by Fish about his struggle with reality... It's not a subject that we felt Fish should be talking about in the first person, so he invented this third-person character. In that way, I suppose you could say it was a concept album.'

That character, Torch, is a novelist trying to write a follow-up to his breakout success – unsubtly representing Fish in the depths of his self-destruction, ravaged by the excesses of fame. A close friend of mine, who would know, has called *Clutching at Straws* the most accurate musical representation of alcoholism he's ever heard – and in fact Side A is as consistent as *Misplaced*, the songs flowing together and recycling themes in a wash of story. It even surpasses its predecessor in places ('Hotel Hobbies' being a superior opening track, for instance). But *Clutching* stumbles on side two. It's not that the songs are bad, only that they break from the disciplined message of the first half, veering through meditations on fame, politics, and long-distance love that work individually but lack coherence – before finally circling back to the motifs of the first half, as though it had been a concept album all along. No wonder Mark and his interviewer found themselves at odds.

'Hotel Hobbies'

The album begins with a sound like a faraway bell or an ice cube clattering in a glass, the low rumble of a synth pad, a meandering bass, long lines of guitar. A quick-rolling keyboard line like a vibraphone sets the tempo for Fish to set the scene: 'hotel hobbies padding dawn's hollow corridors/bellboys checking out the hookers in the bar.' We meet Torch, the character who will be our Virgil for this trip through the circles of Hell, then a long drum roll and a move to the relative major key introduce Torch's 'only sign of life' – his frantic, fevered writing as he 'hide[s] in happy hour.'

The key falls back into the minor for a shredding, snarling guitar solo, but this can't last. The numb vibe of the opening reasserts itself for a final verse as a cruel sun breaks through on a hungover morning, payback for the manic night before, and a lead-in to the expanded view of the next song.

'Warm Wet Circles'

'Warm Wet Circles,' wrote Fish, 'was inspired during a visit to see my parents in North Berwick and spending a night watching the regulars at the Quarterdeck bar in the High Street. I could have been watching Derek Dick at 18 years old.' The lyrics describe the alienated patrons of the bar: local heroes, bored girlfriends, giggling teenagers. They also introduce the 'warm wet circle' motif, cast here as condensation from a glass, a mother's kiss, a bullet hole, a lover's tongue – but ultimately representing the habits of our lives, from social pressures to addiction, that prove so hard to break. Explained Fish, Torch 'watches all the drunks in the bar late at night tracing the circles from their glasses with their fingers – alcoholics always do that!'

The music begins with Steve's classic chiming, slightly delayed arpeggios in a simple F# mixolydian. Ian marks time until the pseudo-chorus, which earns a more committed beat as it establishes a proper F# major tonality that never quite resolves until it falls back into the mixolydian of the verse. Things kick up for the second verse and chorus, then cut away for a sudden bridge established by stabbing piano in the unexpected key of B minor.

The full band returns for a mournful guitar solo, long bends punctuated by sudden bursts of speed. This crashes head-on into a rekeyed bridge, now up at D minor as Fish's voice strains against the tale of one of those teenage girls losing her virginity. This dramatic scene passes as quickly as it came, with the return of the single piano in B minor – the song drawn inexorably backwards in its own circle.

'That Time of the Night (The Short Straw)'

The closest thing the album has to a song suite, and the 'lyric that still reads like my resignation statement' per Fish, begins as a heartbeat bass and tidal synth swells recycle the bridge chords of 'Warm Wet Circles' in E minor. Fish gently describes a lost wedding ring, accompanied by reverb-sunk guitar fills. These become something almost like a solo, though never quite committing, as the heartbeat grows in intensity.

A new section takes over led by a climbing and falling electric piano melody in A mixolydian, setting the scene for Fish's depiction of an insomniac night spent staring at the shadow made by the window frame and wondering where his life is going. The chorus smashes in without a key change, instead cycling back and forth between two chords with no resolution, ending suddenly with a short guitar solo that copies the verse, but in D minor.

The second verse and chorus repeat the pattern but lead to a harsh, amelodic A minor bridge in which the ageing Torch tries to relate to the young bar patrons around him but can't even afford a drink. A chorus sings 'warm wet circles' in stabbing block chords, a taunting version of the refrain that was so sensitive only a song ago. Then suddenly a lone female voice sings it alone over a sloshing delay guitar, her voice watery with flanging, the whole tracking drowning.

'Going Under'

The B-side of 'Incommunicado' doesn't appear on the vinyl or cassette releases of *Clutching at Straws* – but it is on the CD, a bonus track in the middle of the album. Featuring improvised lyrics by Fish over a classic chiming Rothery arpeggio and watery, rumbling synth washes, it's an incredibly dark song. The guitar circles endlessly, recycling the B minor bridge progression from 'Warm Wet Circles,' finding neither climax in a chorus nor release via key change. 'Am I so crazy?' Fish asks at the end, but the song just fades without answers.

One curiosity: during the mastering process, Steve's short, searing guitar solo was left off the CD track. It was neglected again on the 1999 remaster and finally restored only in 2018!

'Just for the Record'

A quick 7/8 keyboard riff opens this song, which quickly shifts to a deep pocketed 7/4 groove in A mixolydian as Fish recounts the familiar theme of the album: 'I'm servin' a sentence to write life's sentences/it's only when I'm out of it I make sense of this.' The song is a study in contrasts, a darkly self-deprecating lyric sung to a catchy tune over an upbeat, major-key arrangement. But it fits the theme, as the title carries a classic Fish double-meaning: 'just so you know, I can quit anytime,' but also 'I'm only destroying myself like this so I can write the new album.'

The groove cuts to a simple half time for the chorus, as Fish/Torch promises he'll quit soon, but the next verse spins up as alluring as ever. The second chorus is twice as long, but still can't hold the line. A half-verse follows, then a short synth lead that brings in a new rhythm, still in a quick 7/8 but with much stricter subdivisions. This stuttering groove smoothes into a seductively simple 4/4 for a proper solo from Mark, then it's back to the intro riff but now in the parallel minor. This leads into another verse, but still in D minor – familiar yet much darker than the start of the song. 'Just for the record, I can stop any day,' Fish promises, the band hits the stuttering 7/8 riff one last time, and then silence.

'White Russian'

'Where do we go from here?' Fish asks over the sound of rushing wind, introducing side two and its hard turn away from the lyrical and musical touchstones of the first half of the album. Written on tour in Austria, 'White Russian' is another of Fish's sadly prescient political lyrics; like 'Fugazi,' it warns of a rising white nationalist tide that has not yet been stemmed. Chilled by the 1986 election of Kurt Waldheim, a former Nazi intelligence officer, to the Austrian presidency, the singer befriended a Jewish-American radio DJ who'd resigned after being warned not to discuss anti-Semitism on air. A day spend observing the city through his eyes led to the lyric and its depictions of 'Uzis on a street corner' – a classic wry Fish irony, considering the Uzi is famously an Israeli gun.

Musically the song earns Fish's description as 'the epic on the album.' It rises through a synth haze into a juddering, syncopated 6/8, like a waltz played backwards, over which Fish spits out his observations. The groove smoothes out for the chorus – 'Where do we go from here?' – but keeps the unsettling sense of rising and falling, all barely-contained energy.

The band drops out for a plaintive bridge as Fish wrestles between ignoring his fears and taking action – finally he decides 'to stand up and fight, I know we have six million reasons.' Over the chorus arrangement, Steve answers the call with a sharp-tongued, blistering solo, then the third verse snaps back into place. The third chorus collapses, spent, into a piano-and-vocal recitation of Fish's desperation to find 'traces of a conscience in residence' in the faces around him. Then comes an outro of the sort not heard since 'Forgotten Sons' – a loping, empty beat underpins a full-band minor-key vamp over which Fish delivers his final challenge to the world to take action before it's too late.

'Incommunicado'

From the sublime to the ridiculous, the tailor-made single of 'Incommunicado' fades in with a pulsing 5/8 groove that gives way to a four-on-the-floor pound under a swirling, virtuosic synth lead. It highlights the break from any 'concept' on side two of *Clutching at Straws* – the lyrics, though drenched in irony as they describe Fish's longing to grow ever more famous, are difficult to fit to the Torch character and ultimately secondary to the simple bounce-along fun of the song.

The verses are delivered over a scorching guitar riff, the pre-chorus cuts to a sparse half-time, then the chorus roars back to life, somehow even bouncier than the verse as Mark goes wild with his right hand under the simple shout-along from Fish. The energy stays high through the second verse and the first concession to Marillion's progressive roots, the curious insertion of a bridge after the verse and before the pre-chorus. That pre-chorus is twice as long as the first, too, maybe not the most commercial choice when radio just wants to get back to the chorus. But we get there, then we get a tight little solo from Mark, then another bridge.

The outro changes things up again, letting Fish sing 'incommunicado' over and over to a new arrangement, but the omnipresent driving beat is still there as the track fades away. Overall, the song is a terrific exercise in writing within the constraints of the radio while changing things up just enough to surprise the listener. It's a clear forefather of the divisive 'Hooks in You,' just as poppy, but just quirky enough for fans to defend it while deriding its offspring.

'Torch Song'

The weak point of *Clutching at Straws* is also its most direct statement. 'Torch Song' reprises the theme of 'Just for the Record,' the question of using one's identity as an artist as an excuse for self-destructive behaviour, but it's a bit on the nose.

The song begins with soft, bell-like plucked guitar, gentle bass and synth pads, and sound effects of laughter and clinking glasses. Fish enters with a curious melody that hovers around the 7th of the E minor key and leaps up a fifth, almost like a bark, in a way unexpected over such a soft arrangement. The rhythm section picks up for a short refrain – 'burn a little brighter now' – into the second verse, which otherwise mimics the first, as does the second refrain, though it repeats a few times before fading away.

The bridge features burbling synths and soft, clean guitar fills under a spoken exchange between Torch and one Dr. Finlay, who advises the singer he'll be dead before 30 if he doesn't slow down, to which the narrator replies that it's 'part of the heritage.' Fish called this breakdown 'a very important part,' adding that he was told the same by his doctor, but since the singer's departure, a few in Marillion's circle have rolled their eyes at the melodramatic pronouncement.

A final verse ups the energy, but just repeats the lyrics from the first; then the last refrain leads to a sombre, stately piano outro, which leads neatly to the intro of the next track. Overall it's a strange song, the vocal at odds with the instrumentation, and perhaps a clue can be gleaned from the demo that appeared on the 2018 *Clutching* remaster. Though the parts are much the same, the playing is much harsher, with a strident tone to the guitar and a thumping bass that overshadows the other instruments with a cutting, almost slap-funk delivery. In this more aggressive setting Fish's melody makes far more sense.

'Slàinte Mhath'

An early sign of Fish's Scottish nationalism (though he had to get the spelling of the title from a friend back home), 'Slàinte Mhath' was inspired by the massive UK miners' strike of 1984-1985 that was eventually broken by Prime Minister Margaret Thatcher. It's a different sort of pub song – painfully self-critical, it finds Fish comparing his own lot as a drunken poet to that of the Scotsmen drinking around him, whose lives are destroyed by the closing of coal mines and industrial centres. Pressured to speak up for them, all he can offer is a trite Gaelic toast: 'good health.'

From a lone piano in G, the band crashes in with grand hits, then falls back to F mixolydian as a loping, open beat and chattering delay guitar take over. Fish delivers his lines in a sneer aimed at himself. A chorus threatens to break out a few times: first with a lone vocal hook ('this is the story so far'), then a sort of pseudo-chorus that collapses when the narrator has nothing better to say than 'slàinte mhath.'

But the song has no real chorus: another verse leads finally to a dynamic leap and a pass through a different key as Fish begs repeatedly, 'take it away, take me away.' Then it's back to F major, though with a new progression, for a climactic final verse decrying the broken promises that have left the workers of Scotland waiting for their jobs to return.

'Sugar Mice'

The closest thing to 'Kayleigh' on *Clutching at Straws* is Fish's tale of a bitter hotel phone call with Tamara while on tour in America. It's much more a pop ballad than 'Kayleigh,' with a slow tempo, simple chords in the guitar-friendly G major, and no key change. In fact, it almost veers into the saccharine (as Fish would on some early solo albums), but is saved by a restrained arrangement that only comes to life halfway through as the drums leap up and Steve delivers one of his greatest solos, aching and lyrical.

'Blame it on me,' Fish insists, and the high fades as the band cuts back for the final verse. Over sparse hats and a sidestick from Ian, the return of the initial guitar arpeggio, and some highly melodic bass fills, Fish retreats to the bar yet again, 'taking a raincheck' from reality rather than face up to his unhappy family at home.

'The Last Straw/Happy Ending'

The straw motif returns in force for the closer, featuring a slow but forceful beat under more chiming guitar. Fish recasts the lyrics of 'Hotel Hobbies' as a suggestion that writing out his troubles helps, a bit, but quickly turns back to the existential political anxieties of side two.

There's not much motion to the lyrics, which mostly recap the main themes, but they're trenchant and well delivered over the snappy verses and cut-time choruses. There's even a call-back to 'Going Under,' with its image of a slaughtered seal, in a murky, rumbling bridge that quotes the tagline of *Jaws 2*: 'just when you thought it was safe to go back to the water...'

The track springs back to life for a throaty guitar solo and the outro. Fish generalises Torch into everyone, or at least the whole band, as he insists, 'If you ever come across us, don't give us your sympathy/you can buy us a drink and just shake our hands.' Then he delivers his final take on the core symbol of the record: 'We're clutching at straws/still drowning.' This becomes a call-and-response between Fish and backup singer Tessa Niles, whose smoky rasp matches Fish's own; they fade out together, shouting back and forth, drowning together.

'Happy Ending,' a sort of gimmicky final track, is simply a voice shouting 'No!' and a long, boozy laugh from Fish.

'Tux On' (B-side of 'Sugar Mice')

A bit of an afterthought, with sparse production and a flat mix, 'Tux On' is nevertheless a fitting B-side for an album about the self-destruction of fame. Based around a quirky cymbal rhythm, a single C minor chord progression, and Fish's meditations on when in life one wears a tuxedo, the song slowly builds towards a central guitar solo that picks up both pace and key with a jump to D minor. This dumps somewhat unceremoniously back into the original key and feel, though bolstered by some funky bass runs through the final chorus fade-out. A bit of an anticlimactic final recording from Fish, it's no wonder that the *B'Sides Themselves* collection broke chronological order to put 'Margaret' last.

Whether the result of newly intense scrutiny or simply a gulf between fan and critic, the press was nowhere near as kind to *Clutching at Straws* as it had been to its predecessor. Claus Nygaard has compiled a long list of damning excerpts from the music papers that had so recently feted Marillion, and the overall impression is of a gigantic yawn.

'I can think of nothing more to say about Marillion than that they sound like Genesis,' wrote *Melody Maker*. 'My father tells me he recognises some early Yes in there,' *NME* sniffed. *Record Mirror* and *Q* may have compared notes: 'Isn't it a bit self-indulgent to make a whole concept album out of the emotional fumblings of your rock'n'roll lifestyle?' asked the former, as the latter said *Clutching* 'could almost be Fish's country and western record, so conspicuously soaked is it in the self-pity that follows straight on the heels of self-indulgence.' The cruellest dig arrived from early champion *Sounds*: 'Back in '77 such stuff was the Enemy, and the kindest thing for Fish and his pseudo band would have been to put them out of their misery with a bullet in the base of the skull. Nowadays, they're such a quaint throwback that I can't get too bothered.'

The tour bus chugged along atop the crazed paving of these mixed messages. Perhaps a smash hit would have papered over the cracks in Marillion, or maybe a vacation would have done what success couldn't. Instead, the band was back on the road.

'The tour bus was not a good place to be,' Fish recalled. 'We all sat in different positions, nobody saying anything. The gang mentality had broken up.' As Mark put it, 'I was going onstage every night and feeling like I was playing by myself. I was up on this big riser away from everybody, and Ian was on this big riser across the stage. You become separated from everything.' Pete added, 'We were in a bit of a bubble. We couldn't go anywhere without security. We had to check into hotels under pseudonyms. We couldn't just go and do a soundcheck.'

As Marillion did Europe, the follow-up single 'Sugar Mice' hit shelves on 13 July. Despite biographer Mick Wall's prediction that it would mark their first #1, 'Sugar Mice' charted at #33 and never even broke the Top 20, peaking at #22 in a seven-week run. Its soft performance did little to bolster the album. Still, Marillion could move tickets, as ably proven by their 18 July show at the Freilichtbühne Loreley in Loreley, Germany, an outdoor headline for some 20,000 fans that was recorded for a VHS release in November and provided lives takes of 'Incommunicado' and 'White Russian' for the B-side of the next single, 'Warm Wet Circles.'

On the 20th Fish and Tamara got married in Haddington, Scotland, with Ian and Privet Hedge as best men. Fish was the last of the band to marry, and hoped that matrimony would provide the stability his fellows had achieved. Instead, the Marillion machine asserted itself once again as Fish and Tamara winged off to Los Angeles at the start of August, their honeymoon postponed in lieu of a round of American promotion.

Borrowing house and car from Marillion's US manager Rod Smallwood, Fish and Tamara made the best of their time in LA. Two weeks passed, but the summons to promote *Clutching at Straws* never arrived. Eventually, it transpired that Capitol, Marillion's distributor in the US, had passed on pushing the album after 'Incommunicado' failed to break. The American tour had been postponed as well – and nobody had told Fish. 'John Arnison never had the balls to tell me that the tour had been put back,' he said. (For Arnison's part, he was busy caring for a very pregnant wife and had trusted Smallwood to keep Fish in the loop.) Fish and Tamara offered to drive cross-country doing radio promo, but Capitol passed on that too, and the newlyweds flew home.

Yet the American tour had only been postponed, not cancelled. So on 16 September, Fish was back in California with the rest of Marillion, watching two trucks full of gear pull up at the 400-capacity Coach House in San Juan Capistrano, down the coast from LA. ('We only unpacked one of them,' Pete recalled.)

Arnison caught up with the band a week later in Boulder, Colorado and discovered a furious Fish waiting for him. The manager's contract was up for renewal and Fish was pushing for his time with Marillion to end. For the most part, the entire band agreed with Fish's complaints: Arnison's drinking was no better than before. (Fish has said he also had a cocaine problem.) The tour carried ridiculous expenses considering what small venues Marillion were playing. Everyone needed a break from the grind.

Worst of all, according to Fish, Arnison took his cut from the band's gross earnings, not their net. In other words, he got paid even when nobody else did, to the extent that Fish has claimed, 'He made three and a half times more than me during 1987-8.' Arnison denies it – 'It was quite simple, if the band did not make money, neither did I' – but Mark has backed up Fish: 'If we toured for a year and didn't make any money, he did... There were tours we did where he didn't take a commission or he took a reduced commission, but if we let him get away with it, he would.'

Fish has claimed that before Arnison arrived in America, he convinced the band and crew to drop the manager and put production manager Andy Field in control of the US tour, going so far as to ready lawyers and accountants in London for the fallout. But when the chips were down, the rest of Marillion backed Arnison.

'They were terrified that I would bring someone else in and turn it into the Fish band,' Fish recalled. Also, Field was seen as an unreliable partier. Fish ultimately attributes the band's decision to Arnison going behind his back, while Arnison attests that 'Steve Rothery was my saviour. He came to me and basically said, "John, you're a great manager, but your drinking is starting to worry us. You need to sort yourself out."'

Whatever ultimately spurred the choice, the die was cast. 'This would be the beginning of the end for me,' Fish recalled, 'as I knew my days were numbered... The rest of the tour was to be the worst in my living memory. I was alienated from the band by their decision and my cards were marked by the manager who now knew of my intentions and realised it was him or me.'

The wall between Fish and the others had become impassable. 'Fish used to disappear into his hotel room and not come out for several days,' remembered Ian. Mark had the opposite problem: 'I remember avoiding Fish on tour. He was in 24/7 party mode. He'd say, "Come on, let's go out." You'd go out, but he wouldn't want you to leave. He'd make you feel like a terrible bastard for wanting to go to bed at 3 am.' The singer lost his voice again in early October, fortunately only for a few days, but it was another period of isolation. The North American tour finally ended on 15 October, with Marillion forced to admit they might never conquer the New World.

Two weeks back home passed as the 'Warm Wet Circles' single released on the 26th. Then it was back to the grind, starting 3 November with three sold-out shows at Wembley Arena, an indoor venue of some 12,000 seats adjacent to Wembley Stadium. The third night was attended by Prince Edward, the 22-year-old son of Queen Elizabeth II. Broadcast on BBC Radio One, the set wound up as the sixth and final disc of the *Early Stages* boxed set; Fish remembers it as a great gig, but the recording suggests otherwise. Marillion sound wooden, and worse, disjointed. Mark's feeling of 'playing by myself' is given life as the instruments slide in and out of time with each other.

'Warm Wet Circles' charted at #40 on 7 November, then repeated the performance of 'Sugar Mice' almost perfectly as it peaked at #22 the next week and hung on for only five more. Meanwhile, the tour ground on through Europe, with heavy coverage of Germany and France. It should have been Marillion's victory lap, selling out across the continent to the largest crowds they'd ever brought in. Instead, Ian said, 'That tour was our most successful, but our most unhappy.'

The whole band was avoiding Fish, who was lost in his misery. Nobody wanted to room with him. 'The realisation of the success he'd craved had left Fish feeling trapped and exploited,' Steve theorised. Ian agreed, 'It was amazing, but Fish took it all for granted.' Pete put it bluntly: 'I hated the tour. I could see the end coming.'

The end, at least of that leg, didn't come until 22 December, when Marillion wrapped up their usual Christmastime run at the NEC in Birmingham. It was backup singer Cori Josias' last show, and more amusingly, the first and last time in his career that Mark tried on a keytar, during the encore of 'Market Square Heroes.' He explained to *The Web*, 'I ended up throwing it in the air because the strap was too short and the mains lead pulled out and it wouldn't work. I got a bit annoyed and slung it on the ground; it seemed the best thing to do at the time.'

1987 was done, but the tour wasn't. More UK dates beckoned, followed by yet another swing through Europe. Biographer Jon Collins has opined that 'hindsight suggests it would have been a good moment to can the tour and salvage the situation.' Instead, Marillion got two weeks for the holidays then got back on the road.

1988: We've Still Got Our Sound

1988 opened with two dark omens of the year to come.
4 January saw the release of *B'Sides Themselves*, a collection of
Marillion's B-sides from 'Grendel' to 'Tux On' – and the first Marillion
release not to chart in the UK, thanks in no small part to EMI's insistence
on releasing the album on CD only. The fans rallied with a campaign
demanding older formats, but those would be months in coming.
Meanwhile, in Aberdeen, Marillion had begun production rehearsals for
the last leg of the tour, where John Arnison, as bad as ever, vomited all
over one of the brand-new stage sets.

Marillion soldiered on, as they always did. The tour resumed in
Aberdeen on the 7th; two nights later in Stoke-on-Trent Fish's voice was
giving out again. They cut 'Market Square Heroes' from the set, but by the
12th Fish was forced to walk on stage in Sheffield and explain to 3,500
expectant fans that he'd lost his voice and the gig was being rescheduled.
He told an MTV interviewer that summer, 'I should have taken nine weeks
off from there, and I didn't... I took three days off.'

Two additional shows had to be rescheduled, but by the 16th Fish
was singing again, just in time for the traditional three in a row at the
Hammersmith Odeon. Then it was again to Europe for a run of seventeen
shows, of which only seven would happen.

The third European tour began in Switzerland on 22 January and soon
headed south for a planned nine shows for Marillion's rabid Italian fans.
Band relations were no better, as Fish continued his vicious cycle of
excess and isolation. 'I'd fallen out with the band who'd lost trust in me
as my escapes became more extreme,' he later wrote. Steve recalled that
Fish 'seemed to be on a mission to self-destruct – something was going
to give.' Ian said simply, 'It was obvious to all of us that things couldn't
continue like that.'

The band and management held numerous emergency meetings
without Fish, who heard them anyway: 'The hotel walls were really thin.
I could hear the band talking about how they were going to replace me.'
His alienation grew, feeding his self-destructive habits:

> The contrast constantly became bigger. You were either in the vocalist's
> camp or you were in favour of the musicians. I had the feeling that
> Marillion had become my accompaniment band; there was nothing left
> of a solid team. I hated this tour. To forget about the problems I started

to booze... With all that stress, you become more susceptible to illness and promptly I got this throat virus. The doctor advised ten weeks of rest, but Mr. Manager told me that this was out of the question because the insurance wouldn't cover the loss. In February 1988 I ended up in hospital, where they told me that if I would do the concert that night, I would have to deal with the after-effects for the rest of my life.

The concert in question was the seventh Italian show, in Modena on 2 February. Once again, Fish could hardly speak. ('The closest I came to a Barry White impersonation,' he later joked.) The gig went on, but Fish heeded the doctor's advice; as fan Luca Benporath described the gig, 'Fish had no voice at all and as he sang that night he was overdubbed by the audience who performed the entire "Lavender" on their own, while Fish left the stage and came into the audience to sing along!'

The day after Modena the tour was mercy-killed and Marillion went home. Prompted by an ultimatum from his long-suffering wife, John Arnison checked in for six weeks of detox at a clinic in Chelsea, who told him his lifestyle was destroying him. (As Mark recalled, 'John told the story of what we had been up to, the clinic recommended that he should get the band in as well!') Fish saw another opportunity to replace the manager he'd grown to hate; after a band meeting at the clinic where they planned for the next tour with John Arnison in a white hospital gown, Fish told the others, 'You're fuckin' mad, this man's in charge of our lives. We've got to get rid of him.' But Marillion, still fearful that a new manager would turn them into Fish's backing band, stayed in Arnison's corner.

EMI exec Dwayne Welch took over as interim manager and the UK shows rescheduled by Fish's lost voice took place in mid-February. March was mercifully light, with just three shows near the end of the month, including the only European show to get rescheduled after the disaster in Modena. This gig in Luxembourg on 29 March was the last indoor show Marillion would play with Fish.

A festival headliner in France on 4 April wrapped up the *Clutching at Straws* tour, which had more sputtered out than climaxed. Fish and Tamara finally got a real honeymoon, heading to the Caribbean for what Fish called 'the first break in a long, long time.' On the 24th, as the singer was tanning on a beach, the rest of Marillion got their first taste of filling his shoes at a fan club event at the Marquee Club where they dropped in to perform 'Market Square Heroes' with fan David Henderson on vocals. May was another quiet month, featuring another last for Marillion: the final time they would play the Aylesbury area with Fish, in the form of a few songs at the wedding of Mark's sister-in-law, until 2007.

Summer was festival season, but it had also been five months since Marillion were last seen on the sales charts and EMI wanted a new album. This time they were 'anxious for new product with an American bent in order to break the only territory that so far had eluded us,' said Fish. So the band buckled in for yet another round of writing sessions, this time in the garage at Pete's farmhouse in Aylesbury, which had been soundproofed by Privet and Andy Field and bore the marked benefit of being free to use.

Things were tense from the word go. 'Our work was becoming a bit too much of a musical backdrop,' Pete recalled. 'It seemed that we would spend months working on stuff, then [Fish would] come in with a lyric he'd just written down the pub and just sing that, so we thought, *Why do we bother?*' Meanwhile Fish felt the others were simply chasing fame by trying to copy *Misplaced Childhood* and its hits. 'I didn't like the music they were making,' he said later. 'It was regressive instead of progressive, simply more and more of the same.'

The sessions were punctuated by two festival gigs that, like the earlier European tours, should have been highlights of Marillion's career. On 11 June, Fish and Mark joined Midge Ure and Phil Collins to perform 'Kayleigh' at the Nelson Mandela 70th Birthday Tribute at Wembley Stadium. (Buoyed by Collins's upbeat drumming and a full horn section, it was perhaps the boppiest version of 'Kayleigh' ever; Ure's take on the solo is also worthy and supposedly earned a nod of approval from Steve in the audience.) A week later, Marillion ventured beyond the Berlin Wall to top the bill at a festival in East Berlin in front of 95,000 people and the cameras of state TV. It was the largest crowd they'd ever headlined, and as Ian recalled, 'The gig was incredible. But we came offstage and [Fish was] saying, "I didn't really enjoy that." That's when alarm bells went off: "If you didn't enjoy that, then something is very wrong..."'

Nor was writing at Pete's working. Hoping to move things along, Marillion booked time at Tone Deaf, a demo studio in Wallingford, thinking recording the bits and pieces they'd cooked up thus far might transform them into real songs. The sessions, which Fish only attended once to put down his vocals, produced a handful of demos: 'Story From a Thin Wall,' 'Shadows on the Barley,' 'Sunset Hill,' and 'Tic-Tac-Toe.' But they were little more than ideas and put Marillion no closer to a record.

Fish, still clinging on, proposed a solution: decamp to Victorian-era

Dalnaglar Castle in the Scottish Highlands and lock themselves away from the real world. The others agreed and in mid-July they headed north with Andy Field in tow.

Fish later said, 'The first two weeks went fine. The atmosphere was great and we wrote excellent music.' But romantic Dalnaglar couldn't solve the problems of Pete's garage. 'The band was unsatisfied with my lyrics,' Fish recalled. Some pieces were influenced by his growing interest in Scottish Nationalism while others took shots at American greed. 'I heard immediately from all sides: "No, don't do that! We need America."' He was critical of the music in return: 'We went back to the same routine. It was the same bits going up on the fucking blackboard: this is the Joni Mitchell section, this is the Floyd section. There we were again, in the same shit.' He told the others, 'I can't write over this – I need to have some sort of structure.'

Meanwhile, EMI had caved to fan pressure and released *B'Sides Themselves* on cassette and vinyl on 11 July. They were rewarded with a brief swing through the charts, as the compilation album entered the rankings at #64 on the 23rd and took five more weeks to slide off. But 23 July marked a second, much darker milestone in Marillion's history: the band's final show with Fish.

Fife Aid 2, a charity festival organized by TV naturalist David Bellamy, took place at Craigtoun Country Park not far from Dalnaglar, and Fish finagled the band into attending. 'He told John Arnison that we were into it, then told us that John was into it,' Mark explained. By the end of the gig, nobody was into it. Steve called it 'a fairly dismal day all around.' To Fish it was 'a remarkable disaster... Our gig was tired and angry and the hotel après show was a cauldron of hate as everyone blamed me for the decision to play.' He added, 'I always regret not doing what David Bowie did at the Hammy Odeon... going on saying, "Well this is the last gig I'm ever going to do" and not telling the band.'

Nonetheless, the possibility of salvaging Marillion still hung tantalisingly before all their faces. Back at Dalnaglar a few more lyrics and bits of music were recorded, but the band had balkanised into two camps: Fish and everyone else. As the singer put it, 'It was confrontation after confrontation and rather than bring us together again we separated. I was in the tower with the drugs and the crew while the band was downstairs with their stash, both parties slagging off the other.'

Tensions rose when artist Mark Wilkinson sent up a cover proposal for a book he and Fish were planning about the art of Marillion. Fish had tasked John Arnison with informing the rest of the band about the project, but Marillion didn't get the word and Wilkinson's package caught them by surprise. 'We thought Fish was going behind our backs,' Pete recalled. 'Fish appeared to want the rest of the world to think that Marillion was him, and that was unacceptable to the rest of us.'

'That was a terrible mistake,' Mark ultimately said of Dalnaglar. 'Not only were we not getting on, we didn't really want to be together, and we had nowhere to go.' So the confining castle was abandoned at the end of August and Marillion returned south with 'two or three good ideas out of 20,' as Mark put it. Back in Aylesbury Fish worked on lyrics by himself, or occasionally with friends outside Marillion, as the others prepared music together. 'Fish would turn up very occasionally; he just wasn't interested,' Ian recalled. As Mark put it, 'He used to stay long enough to tell us the music we were working on was "shite" and then leave. To be fair, we were as complimentary about the lyrics he showed us.'

Meanwhile, EMI courted Bob Ezrin for the album, hoping the legendary producer of Pink Floyd's *The Wall*, Kiss's *Destroyer*, and Alice Cooper's *Welcome to My Nightmare* could help Marillion break America. In early September Ezrin stopped by Tone Deaf to hear what Marillion had worked up. As Fish tells it,

He said, 'OK, play me what you've got.' And the band played all the bits and pieces they had. And Bob said, 'There are no songs here. These are just bits.' After Bob left, the band started going, 'Alright, let's try joining this bit onto this bit.' And I just went, 'This is a waste of fucking time. I can't deal with it.'

Unsurprisingly Fish liked Ezrin, who encouraged him to explore his new songwriting themes. The others, not so much. 'I had huge respect for Bob Ezrin until I met him,' Pete recalled. 'He didn't really like what we had done; he said it was stuff we could knock out in our sleep. But when he sat at the piano and showed us what he might do, it was much too Andrew Lloyd Webber!'

Ian found him 'barking mad – in a good way.' He also claimed Ezrin said of Fish, 'I wish he'd get off this T S Elliott [sic] trip he's on,' but ultimately it didn't matter whose camp Ezrin landed in – a week after his meeting with Marillion, the band would fall apart.

The summer's work eventually saw the light of day on the two-disc remaster of *Clutching at Straws* EMI released in 1997. As painful as it is to admit, if they make an accurate record of the direction Marillion's fifth album was headed with Fish involved, it may have been best that the split happened when it did. The demos sound exactly as both Fish and the others have described: the singer delivering underdeveloped lyrics over underdeveloped musical ideas, with almost no connection between the two. The careful prosody of Marillion's work up to that time, in which the music thoughtfully reflects and reinforces the words, is almost completely absent, replaced by ill-fitting lines forced into the shape of backing tracks.

Almost all the musical ideas on the demos were reworked (and much improved) as the songs on *Seasons End*, Marillion's post-Fish debut, while many of the lyrics and concepts saw use on Fish's solo albums. Musically, 'Story from a Thin Wall' was used almost wholesale as 'Berlin,' 'Shadows on the Barley' and 'Tic-Tac-Toe' became the B-sides 'The Bell in the Sea' and 'The Release' respectively, and the earlier 'Beaujolais Day,' which hadn't made the cut for *Clutching at Straws*, turned into 'Seasons End.' 'Sunset Hill' was split neatly in the divorce: the music turned into Marillion's 'The King of Sunset Town' and the lyric went to Fish's 'View from the Hill' and later, 'Fortunes of War.' He also took the 'Story from a Thin Wall' lyric for 'Family Business,' bits from 'Voice in the Crowd' for 'Vigil,' 'Tic-Tac-Toe' for his debut single 'State of Mind,' and 'Exile on Princes Street' for the excellent 'Internal Exile.'

But that was all to come. As September of 1988 ground on, another fight broke out over Mark Wilkinson, this time between Fish and Mark Kelly regarding ownership of Wilkinson's original paintings for the band, which Fish demanded all of. A band meeting at Fish's house only made things worse, as the singer felt betrayed yet again: 'The band met with John [Arnison] at Ian's before and arrived with what seemed a pre-determined agenda.' Furious, Fish headed for his cousin's place in Gerrards Cross, where he tried his best to black out: 'I drunk a 40-fluid-oz bottle of Jim Beam on my fucking own, and I was still standing, because I was so stressed and tense.' His immunity to Kentucky bourbon surprised even Fish. '[A] little voice went off in the back of my head: "You're gonna kill yourself." I realised I was in a very dangerous area.'

Eventually Fish slept, and when he woke the next day it was with a new, furious clarity: 'I wrote a five-page letter, got it photocopied at a local office suppliers and paid for a taxi driver to deliver it to everybody else's house. I basically said, "Either fundamental changes are made within the management and we get rid of John Arnison, or I'm leaving."'

Steve, Mark, Pete, and Ian shared a round of phone calls as each discovered the letter in his mailbox. Their reactions to the letter ranged from exhaustion to relief – surprise was notably absent. 'Fish said he wanted 50 per cent of all the publishing and all the writing,' Ian recalled. 'That's when it got out of hand. Everybody said, "This has gone too far."' Steve, meanwhile, felt that 'Fish had never really had anything to do with the writing of the music. So we knew that our musical identity was still there... Maybe, slightly naïvely, we thought it would be just a case of finding someone to replace him. As if it was ever going to be that easy.' Pete's response to the idea of replacing Fish was similar: 'OK, this is part of the process.' But as Ian summed it up, 'everyone's response was the same – "Well, he can just fuck off!"'

Mark remembers Fish coming back to Arnison a few days later to say he might have been too hasty, though the singer denies this. Either way, it was all over, as Fish was swiftly informed his services would no longer be needed. ('It was John who phoned me and said the band wouldn't accept my terms for remaining in the band, one of which was John's removal from office,' he later wrote.) In mid-September EMI released a statement to the press as Fish released one of his own, featuring the usual bland language: 'I've had a brilliant seven years with Marillion; however, recently the musical directions of the band have diversified to such an extent I realised the time had come to embark on a solo career.' The band's own message to fanzine *The Web* was similarly a masterpiece of restraint: 'During the process of writing the new album it became apparent that differences, both musically and lyrically, between Fish and the rest of the band were irreconcilable.'

As barbs from both sides flew in the press in what Fish called 'a very public and very angry divorce,' the now singerless Marillion carried on as best they could. Just as after the departure of Doug Irvine in 1980, there was no talk of ending the band. 'We felt that the band had a very strong musical identity, and we believed very much in what we wanted to do,' recalled Steve. 'We never even considered the possibility of splitting up or stopping what Marillion was. It was too much of our lives.' Added Mark, 'There was never any question of us not carrying on. Fish was the public face of Marillion... but at the end of the day it is the music people listen to when they buy a record – and we've still got our sound. It was the four of us that made that sound!'

All upcoming tour dates were cancelled aside from a half-hour instrumental set by Steve at a mid-September guitar clinic in Holland and two fan club gigs in Utrecht and Liverpool. At the first, on 12 November,

Pete led the crowd as they sang a few songs together. Meanwhile, EMI had put together a live record, *The Thieving Magpie*, to serve as Fish's farewell (and buy the band a bit of time to regroup). Overdubs, performed with Nick Davis at Westside, were carefully scheduled so that Fish never overlapped with the rest of the band.

Spanning nearly the entire Fish era of Marillion, *Magpie* featured hits and deep favourites from all four albums and saw the remaining four band members doing promo that mostly consisted of explaining Fish's departure rather than pushing the new release. ('SO LONG AND THANKS FOR ALL THE (LYRICS) FISH' blared the cover of the 26 November *Kerrang!* over a picture of Mark, Steve, and an empty fish tank.) The single, a live version of 'Freaks,' was released on 21 November and hit #24 that week, but lacked legs. The album came out on the 29th and entered the charts at #25 in early December, but was gone by mid-January – though it did sell well enough to earn both silver and gold certs upon release.

10 December saw Dave Lloyd of Rage handle vocal duties for the Liverpool fan-club show. ('It went down surprisingly well,' Mark recalled, 'especially considering that Dave didn't know any of the songs.') But Marillion couldn't let fans and friends sing forever, not if they were to meet their contractual duties to EMI and produce a new album in 1989. Nor would a mere vocalist be enough, since in losing Fish Marillion had lost their frontman and lyricist as well.

Starting in November the band placed ads in all the usual music mags: 'MARILLION REQUIRE VOCALIST,' read an ad in *Melody Maker*. 'Please send tape, biog, and photo... Only serious applications please.' They received some 300 tapes in return and pored through them seeking any possible fit. The best of the bunch, about 30 singers, were invited to audition at old Marillion haunts Nomis and Westside. 'We had some hilarious rehearsals,' Pete recalled. 'People would dance around – one guy even acted out 'Fugazi' word for word!'

Between the wide net they cast and their connections into the burgeoning neo-prog scene they'd spearheaded, Marillion should have had no trouble finding their new voice, but the band were well aware that simply picking the best Fish clone would be the kiss of death. Pete again: 'It was quite obvious when we started auditioning people what they thought we wanted... It wasn't a case of knowing what we wanted, but of knowing what we didn't want.' Moreover, whoever earned the spot had to be an equal contributor, not just a voice who would do as he was told, as shown by the decision to give prospective singers a shot at the new material. As Stuart Nicholson of neo-prog band Galahad described his own failed audition, 'We played "Kayleigh," "Lavender," "Blue Angel," "Slàinte Mhath," "Forgotten Sons" and a lot of jammed new material with me frantically trying to find lyrics that fitted the music.'

Meanwhile, Marillion and team undertook a separate hunt for a lyricist, figuring they could work words into music themselves (with Pete singing at the writing sessions) until they settled on a singer to put the final polish on. Of the various writers they tried, Marillion clicked best with EMI-suggested John Helmer, frontman of the Brighton post-punk band The Piranhas. 'John was the one lyricist who stood out to me,' Steve said. 'It was so different to the stuff Fish was doing – good, strong, colourful imagery, but emotionally very direct.'

The guitarist met Helmer in London and tasked him to put words to a composition inspired by Marillion's time in Berlin. Despite never having been to the city in question, Helmer's effort was strong enough to earn him an invitation to Aylesbury to meet the rest of the band. There, Mark and Steve briefed him on their lyrical ideas without playing him any music and asked him to come back with something usable.

Incredibly, it worked: 'My lyrics struck the right chord,' Helmer remarked at the time, 'something that really amazed me because they were born out of a completely different style of music.' In addition to the first draft of 'Berlin,' Helmer completed 'Seasons End' over Christmas – 'exactly as it is on the album,' Steve said.

Vocal auditions continued with would-be singers working from Helmer's drafts, which barely helped. 'We had two tunes,' said Mark, '"The Release" and "King of Sunset Town." We had some lyrics from John Helmer. It was a test of their voice and their approach. It was amazing how different singers, given nothing but a semi-blank canvas, half of them can't actually do it!'

There would be no Christmas tour in 1988, nor a singer to put Helmer's words to Marillion's music. But unbeknownst to the band, Santa Claus had already delivered their gift in the form of a demo tape from singer-songwriter Steve Hogarth – even if the voice they'd been waiting for wouldn't be unwrapped until after the new year.

1989: Coming In Out of the Cold

Fish wasn't wasting any time.
As Marillion sought his replacement, the singer got his solo debut
underway. Under the management of John Cavanagh, an ex-EMI exec
whom Fish had suggested as John Arnison's replacement, he was content
to stay with EMI. For their part, the label was eager to see if Marillion
could earn one more Genesis comparison by spinning off a singer into his
own hit act.

The pay was less than with Marillion, but Fish was 'eager to prove
[himself] as a successful solo act, sell a shed full of albums and go back
and renegotiate a better deal for the second solo project.' So early 1989
found Fish with a slew of songs ready for the studio, co-written mostly
with keyboardist Mickey Simmonds, who lived near Fish and had worked
on a number of ideas with him intended for the fifth Marillion album.
Instead, Fish and Simmonds put together a band of session players.
Armed with an advance from EMI, Fish's goal was to get a record out, get
back on the road, and be selling as many albums and concert tickets as
Marillion by summer of 1990.

Meanwhile, Marillion were still digging through a pile of audition
tapes. Music publishers Rondor, who had been part of the search for
lyricists in late 1900, had also built a good relationship with a singer
songwriter named Steve Hogarth, late of The Europeans and How We
Live. Disillusioned after the mistreatment of How We Live by label CBS,
and with a young family to support, Hogarth was considering anything
that might offer a steady paycheck: 'I didn't want to be a musician
anymore. I was in the process of jacking it all in, selling our little house in
Windsor. We were going to ... live a quiet life and get real again.' He even
considered becoming a milkman. Steve's story continues:

> Just before Christmas 1988, I was in the office of Rondor, my publishers,
> and asked if anyone had anything I could do – I meant in the office, a
> bit of typing, or engineering their little demo studio... Being Christmas,
> everyone was hung over from a party. The general manager, Alan Jones,
> lifted his head up off a sofa in his office and said: 'Do you know Marillion
> are looking for a singer?' I said: 'I didn't mean that.'

Egged on by violinist Darryl Way of Curved Air, Hogarth let the publisher
send a cassette to Marillion containing three or four of his songs: 'Games in

Germany,' 'Til Kingdom Come,' 'Easter,' and possibly 'Burning Inside You.' At the start of 1989, Ian Mosley popped it into the tape deck of his car on a drive to Pete's house. As he tells it, 'I used to put them in the cassette player whilst I was driving out of Aylesbury to Pete's and usually listen to half a number and throw them into the back seat and put the next in... I opened the envelope and there was a photo of Steve Hogarth. I thought he was a good looking boy. I put the cassette in and it was 'Games in Germany' and straight away I thought he had a great voice. There was something I could really identify with in that track too.'

Ian played the tape for the others, who agreed immediately that Hogarth should be brought in. John Arnison recalled, 'I listened to the tape and thought, that's the voice,' while Steve explained, "When we heard "Games in Germany" from Steve's tape it was "Oh, intelligent lyrics, great vocal performance, a lot more of a singer." It was obvious he was working in a similar musical vein, and his voice seemed really quite distinct.'

Dwayne Welch, still in the manager's seat, reached out to Hogarth, who'd forgotten all about Marillion – and just been asked to play piano on tour with art-rocker Matt Johnson's band The The, having contributed keys to their 1986 hit *Infected*. (Hogarth has often joked since that he 'had to make a choice between the most hip band in the world and the least.') The singer declined to audition, but Welch kept at it, and eventually, Hogarth agreed to meet Marillion at Pete's house.

When he showed up on 24 January – a day late thanks to his car being stolen, and viciously allergic to Pete's cats – the band was confronted with someone totally unlike Fish in every way. If Fish was a drunken court jester, Hogarth had the suave polish of a stage magician. Elfin where Fish was gigantic, with the thick hair, deep eyes, and razor jaw of a teen heartthrob, he was the perfect face for Marillion to present to the impending nineties. His voice contrasted, too; he could hit all Fish's notes, but while the great Scotsman entered the stratosphere via his flutey falsetto, Hogarth did it with a tight-throated wail. And unlike Fish, Hogarth was a trained musician, capable on piano and guitar, with numerous songwriting credits under his belt.

It was an audition for Marillion, too, who at first failed to impress. Thanks to Pete's cats the band had set up in the garage, Hogarth recalled: 'It was just ridiculous, like all the gear in the world crammed into an outside toilet... It was a bit like cramming into the back room of a music shop.' Meanwhile, Mark was put off, sensing that Hogarth felt himself too good for the whole prog business.

Thus relations were shaky until Hogarth asked Marillion what, exactly, they were looking for: 'I expected them to say, "We're this big progressive rock band and we sell this many copies. It's a good living, and do you think you can sing like this?" I would have gone, "Well, no," and "Cheers," and that would have been the end of it.'

Instead, Hogarth recalls, he was told,

'We've heard these songs that you've written and we've heard what you sing, and we just want you to do what you do, and we'll do what we do, and let's see what happens.' So it was presented to me as an experiment to start with, that they were obviously completely willing to move forward naturally, with a different human being doing different things at the front. So there wasn't any kind of reference to what had gone before; they just said, 'Be yourself.'

The band handed Hogarth printouts of John Helmer's lyrics and asked him to try them out over the music they'd worked up. One was a lyric called 'King of Sunset Town,' which Hogarth sang over an iteration on the 'Sunset Hill' demo from the year before. 'They gave me a lyric sheet and said "We'll play this idea we've been jamming around, and do you want to sing these words?"' Hogarth said. 'There wasn't a tune, they just told me to make one up. So I took a deep breath, listened to what they were doing and did it.'

Hogarth has since sworn he was out of tune, but Steve Rothery remembered instant magic: 'By 20 minutes of us playing together, it sort of existed as a song. It was evident immediately that we'd work together – creativity was effortless.' He added, 'The minute Steve started singing, it was like our whole creativity became supercharged again. It had that same magic, working together, that we'd had in the early days with Fish, and it was obvious to us all, right from the word go, that this was the guy for the job.'

At the end of the day, Marillion offered Hogarth a probationary period, inviting him to continue writing and rehearsing with them as they prepped the new album. To the band's surprise, the singer again demurred, asking for a week to think it over. ('I remember being pissed off that he kept us waiting for a week while he made his mind up,' said Mark.) But Marillion didn't just cross their fingers; they called up their contacts and per Mark, 'said, "Listen, bend his ear a bit, 'cos we really want him to join." Or as Ian put it: 'I rang Darryl [Way] up and told him that we really wanted Steve to join the band and I asked him if there was anything we could do. Can we send his wife some flowers?' In the end, it worked. Hogarth explained what swayed his decision:

First of all meeting the boys, they're really nice people. Matt from The The is very intense; he's not much fun. What really swung it, the hard-headed part was that it was really the difference between going and playing for somebody for seven months then saying goodbye or becoming part of something that would be as much about me as anything else. I'm a creative person, and this was a chance to weld myself on to Marillion, instead of just working for somebody.

So Hogarth met Marillion and engineer/producer Nick Davis at the Music Farm, a rehearsal studio based in a former mushroom farm in Brighton, for a two-week stab at recapturing the electricity of his audition. *The Web* wrote, 'Obviously, the news that everyone is waiting for is who is the new singer? At this stage all I can say is the group are locked in a rehearsal studio with Steve Hogarth... At the moment, all appears to be going well; however, no final decision has yet been made so I cannot confirm either way.'

'Going well' was an understatement: 'That was such a creative time,' Steve Rothery recalled. 'The adrenalin was really going, it was incredible.' For his part, the new Steve described joining Marillion as 'like coming in out of the cold.'

From the first, Hogarth was treated like a full member of the band. 'I guess I was "on trial,"' he said, 'although I wasn't made to feel so. During the day we would jam and record, and at night when we'd had enough, we'd either stay in and play pool whilst listening to the day's jams, or we'd drive into Brighton and find a vibey place to get slightly sloshed and talk rubbish! I grew to love the boys in a very short space of time.'

Marillion continued to encourage Hogarth's contributions and even offered the same contract they had. 'You got the immediate impression that he wasn't joining them,' Privet Hedge recalled, 'they were joining each other.' Or as Hogarth put it, 'It all seemed very, very fair, especially considering that they were already famous selling bucket loads of records and I wasn't.' He signed with EMI on 2 February.

Almost all of *Seasons End* was written and demoed at the Music Farm. Much of the work involved putting Helmer's lyrics to Marillion's demos, but there was room for the new as well. 'Holloway Girl' was written around a lyric of Hogarth's; 'Hooks in You' came together in 'about an hour,' per Hogarth, after he heard Steve's guitar riff through the kitchenette wall. Also, when he came to the Farm, the singer brought along a red plastic bucket full of demo tapes from his time with his previous bands. 'If we ran out of ideas the boys would say, "Have you got anything in the bucket?"' he explained. 'I'd take out a cassette and say, "What do you think?"'

Gems from the red bucket contributed much of 'The Space' and, most famously, 'Easter,' which Hogarth had written on a trip to Belfast. Marillion had heard it before, on Hogarth's audition tape, but now it took on new life. They ended up adding not only the long 5/4 outro, but Steve's beloved guitar solo: 'This guitar solo just seemed to grow out of nothing,' Pete recalled. 'Luckily we were recording it onto a Portastudio and that very solo was the one we later got Steve to re-learn and play for the album.'

As Marillion broke in the new guy, Fish was the first to get back on the road with a 21 March warm-up gig in Lockerbie, Scotland. By April, Marillion and their ex-singer were head to head working on their respective albums. Fish entered Townhouse Studios in London with Jon Kelly, who had co-produced Kate Bush's #1 album *Never for Ever*, and on the 28th Marillion set up shop at Hook End Manor Studios, a residential recording studio based in a luxurious sixteenth-century house in Oxfordshire.

Work on *Seasons End* was quick and mostly painless. 'It was just like being on holiday,' Ian recalled. 'We just played tennis every day and built hot-air balloons.' The only intrusion of cold reality came in the form of legal action by Fish, asserting that he owned a fifth of the band's equipment, to the extent that at one point the police showed up to serve an injunction demanding they stop recording. ('We videoed it; asked them to get the handcuffs and truncheon out,' recalled Hogarth. 'It was a scream. Legally he couldn't stop me recording, just the band, so I just went in and did vocals for a couple of days while we overturned the writ.') Ultimately both parties were advised to settle out of court.

Recording at Hook End continued through May and into June, which also saw Hogarth's first performance with Marillion, a warm-up gig following the band tradition of small, secret shows under goofy names – this time as 'Low Fat Yogurts' at the Crooked Billet in Stoke Row. A historic pub near Hook End, the Crooked Billet was chosen for Hogarth's debut after the barman and a slightly drunk Mark agreed the band really ought to play there. The band's hasty practice sessions were terrible at first but soon came together, and on 8 June Hogarth took the stage in front of about a hundred fans crammed into one tiny room (with a hundred more outside in the rain and peering in the windows).

Hogarth was terrified, both by the pressure of his debut and the packed crowd that, with no security or barriers, towered over his five-seven frame. But he 'fronted it out,' as he put it in an interview soon after, 'and it was a great success.' Marillion split their set between five old tracks and five that would soon arrive on the new album; then, with their set complete and the crowd still packed into every inch of the Crooked Billet, the only way out was through a window behind the stage.

Soon Marillion moved to Westside in London for final overdubs and mixing, but by the end of June Fish outpaced them again by completing his *Vigil in a Wilderness of Mirrors* – only to learn that EMI was putting it on ice. Wary of splitting up profits or chart positions, they intended to let Marillion have 1989 and hold onto Fish's debut until 1990. The singer would ultimately point the finger at this decision as one of the major causes of the financial woes that would soon befall him.

But for Marillion, things were looking rosy. On August 1st they shot the video for 'Hooks in You,' an easy choice for the lead single with its killer riff, shoutalong chorus, and driving beat reminiscent of 'Incommunicado.' (Though Mark has since said, 'Almost any other song would have been a better advert for the album and new line-up.') Before a bouncing crowd of fans at Brixton Academy Theatre in London, Steve Hogarth made his official debut with his nerves even more jangled than they'd been at the Crooked Billet:

I was a trembling nervous wreck because it was my first time ever in front of about 600 Marillion fans and unless you've been to a Marillion concert, or you are a Marillion fan, then you don't really know the level of fanaticism and dedication that these people have ... I thought, 'Well, if they're gonna murder me then there's cameras here to witness the whole event as well.' But I shouldn't have worried, because they were actually chanting my name as I walked onstage, which amazed me. I thought they were actually chanting for Steve Rothery!

The band mimed their way through 'Hooks in You' about a dozen times, and between shoots, Marillion signed autographs, answered questions, led a cappella singalongs of old tunes, and even performed an acoustic version of the upcoming B-side 'After Me.' Hogarth came away impressed by the fans who brought a party atmosphere to the shoot and seemed to only grow more enthusiastic as the long day wore on:

> [The fans] were shepherded into this gig, and they're getting this song blasted at them they've never heard before, by their favourite band ... with a new singer that I don't suppose they knew if they'd like or not. When you make a video, you're stopping and starting, playing things back over and over again. The third or fourth time they played it back they knew it then!

The finished video was a stark departure from Marillion's usual. It's a simple faux-live affair – with terrific energy – intercut via a jagged animal-claw effect with glamour shots of a model in a tattered wedding dress. It's Marillion as hair band, down to Steve Rothery's cut-off leather jacket and Charvel guitar. Mark offered this explanation: 'What's happened is that in the past we've always wanted to do live videos, but Fish saw videos as a vehicle for his acting aspirations. We all felt that one of the strongest areas of the band was playing live. When Steve joined, it seemed the most logical thing to do.'

The single hit shelves a few weeks later, on 29 August. Despite everything – the radio-friendly sound, the slick video and its telegenic new singer, the legions of fans eager for word of their favourite band – 'Hooks in You' was, by Marillion standards, a flop. It charted at #32 on 9 September, hit #30 the next week, then slid to #52 and disappeared.

Then it was time for *Seasons End*, which arrived on 25 September. For the first time, a Marillion release featured a cover by someone other than Mark Wilkinson, who had gone with Fish in the split. Graphic artist Carl Glover designed a photomontage featuring four frames that suggest the four seasons or elements, while also slyly putting an end to the band's old symbols: a magpie's feather floats down to a barren desert; the peak of a jester's cap stands lonely below an empty sky; a chameleon is silhouetted against raging flames; a painting of a clown sinks into a lake.

Seasons End wound up making another reference to early Marillion history: on 7 October, as the band set out for its first tour with its new frontman, the album entered the charts at #7. But unlike *Script for a Jester's Tear*, which had done the same in 1983, *Seasons End* couldn't hold on to the Top 10, or even the Top 20. It spent a mere four weeks on the charts, sliding from #21 through #41 to #68 before dropping off. Presales had been enough for a silver certification a few days after release, but it seemed that with the departure of Fish, Marillion's appeal had contracted severely.

Seasons End

Personnel:
Steve Hogarth: vocals
Steve Rothery: guitars
Pete Trewavas: bass
Mark Kelly: keyboards
Ian Mosley: drums
Additional musicians:
Phil Todd: saxophone on 'Berlin'
Jean-Pierre Rasle: pipes on 'Easter'
Nick Davis: co-producer
Release date: 25 September 1989
Highest chart places: 7 (UK)
Running time: 47:35 (LP), 50:56 (CD)

Steve Hogarth's Marillion debut is one of his best, but it's not without flaws. Chief among them is the likely result of the difficult songwriting and process, during which the band worked up most of the music under the pressure of their looming break with Fish, then tasked Hogarth with fitting John Helmer's lyrics over it all. Meanwhile, Nick Davis, who'd engineered *Clutching at Straws*, was now in the producer's chair for the first time. The result is an album consisting of eight (or nine, on the CD) strong songs that have a little too much in common, sonically and structurally.

A number of arranging tics are repeated across *Seasons End* – the opening arpeggio and quiet starting verses, the sudden build-up to the chorus or refrain, the bridge that strips back to just a synth pad, the end-of-song fadeout. Sounds are reused, too, most egregiously the twelve-string acoustic guitar on 'Easter' and 'After You.' All the pieces work in any given song, but their reuse becomes a bit numbing, making the tracks run together in a way that doesn't do justice to their individual strengths.

'The King of Sunset Town' (Hogarth/Rothery/Kelly/Trewavas/Mosley/Helmer)
A long, long swell of washing, glittering synths and pulsing bass – nearly two minutes – preludes Steve Hogarth's debut. The band tightens up

around the sudden onset of Ian's drums for a glorious guitar solo, which fades into a classic Rothery arpeggio, a bit more syncopated than usual. Finally, two and a half minutes in, we hear Hogarth's voice for the first time. (Apparently, the song was chosen as the opener on the first tour so the audience could have some time with the band they knew and loved before the new singer came onstage.)

The lyric as written by John Helmer told of life among the homeless, but Hogarth tweaked it last-minute into a celebration of the man who stood alone against a line of Chinese tanks the day after their bloody suppression of the Tiananmen Square protests on 4 June 1989. Two soft verses lead to a chorus delivered in Hogarth's characteristic full-bore rasp, swooping between registers over stuttering drums, their lines about the turning wheel of history equally mournful and triumphant. The basic pattern repeats, extended by an extra refrain and a reprise of the guitar solo, then falls back for a third verse over echoing, clanging piano stabs. This builds back again into a final long chorus, which repeats over a 30-second-long fade to black.

'Easter' (Hogarth/Rothery/Kelly/Trewavas/Mosley)

Hogarth's signature ballad makes a perfect contrast with 'Forgotten Sons.' Both are about the Troubles in Northern Ireland, but they couldn't be more different. Hogarth's lyric, inspired by William Butler Yeats's poem 'Easter, 1916' about the Irish Easter Rising, is gentle and hopeful: 'Easter, surely now can all of your hearts be free.' The lilting music, inspired by the Jacobite anthem 'Skye Boat Song,' only underlines the singer's compassion.

The chords are simple, like a folksong, keeping to the guitar-friendly G major for the verse and chorus and only moving decisively to the relative E minor after the second chorus for a short, flutey synth lead and then a guitar solo that has earned decades of well-deserved praise from fans. Swelling into being, rising and falling, crashing and receding as the band dynamic builds, it's Steve Rothery at his melodic best.

As the guitar dissolves into whining feedback a new rhythm appears, a gently rolling 5/4 groove that Marillion added to the song at Mushroom Farm to provide a hint of anxious melancholy: 'What will you do with the wire and the gun/That'll set things right when it's said and done?' This section repeats until, with the guitar swelling and stacked backing vocals providing a lush descant, 'Easter' fades with its questions unanswered.

'The Uninvited Guest' (Hogarth/Rothery/Kelly/Trewavas/Mosley/Helmer)

A martial, start-and-stop beat and an uncharacteristically amelodic arpeggio from the guitar underpin a lyric that drips with wry sarcasm, from the perspective of unwanted intruders of all sorts who disrupt one's life. John Helmer has also said the lyric was surreptitiously about the AIDS epidemic of the eighties and the death of the free-love era, though the more humorous reading is supported by lines like 'I'm your fifteen-stone first-footer.'

Fifteen stone is a classically eccentric British way of measuring 210 pounds, while a first-footer is, in Scottish tradition, the first person to enter one's house in the New Year, who must be plied with food and drink. It's traditionally good luck for the first-footer to be a tall, dark-haired man – one guess at the object of satire here. (A clue: 'It was originally eighteen-stone first-footer,' per Mark, 'but Steve Rothery said he thought it was a bit much.')

The chorus – written to get crowds going – leaps to life with a stomping beat, slashing power chords and a bouncy synth arpeggio. The bridge drops down to just a synth wash, then swells with full-band hits and a fleet-fingered, if buried, guitar lead, then cycles back to an even more pounding arrangement of the chorus. A return to the bridge progression heralds a proper guitar solo, Steve at his absolute shreddiest, which crashes to a conclusion with just the synth arpeggio and a cuckoo-clock hoot to fade away.

'Seasons End' (Hogarth/Rothery/Kelly/Trewavas/Mosley/Helmer)

The title track of *Seasons End* is also its least inspired, with some blocky dynamics and an unnecessary eight-minute length. John Helmer's global-warming lyric, while well intentioned, is a bit on the nose ('Snowflakes in a new-born fist/sledging on a hill/are these things we'll never see in England?').

A soft arpeggio reminiscent of 'Going Under' opens the track, supporting two verses in C minor as synth pads grow underneath. The chorus keeps the same key and basic arrangement, just a bit bigger, with a new progression, a wider spread from the keys, and more attack on the guitar. It falls back a bit for another verse, rises for the next chorus, then finally blooms into a guitar solo over the verse progression and a symphonic keyboard line over the chorus. The dynamic stays up for the next chorus, with searing guitar leads providing counterpoint, finally landing back on the C minor root as the song fades into its second half.

It's taken until the five-minute mark for the groove and tempo to change, and even the transition feels a bit stitched together.

The long outro of 'Seasons End' was layered in the studio and took Marillion a while to tackle live. It begins with a single palm-muted guitar playing a clicky 7/8 ostinato. The rest of the band rises beneath, playing mostly in the same time signature save for a polyrhythm from one of the synth voices. Time becomes slippery until somehow we've moved to a straight-ahead 4/4, Pete pulsing out eighth notes on the bass and Ian slowly building up the drums then letting them fall away, but without any resolution, as the track simply fades on this final groove.

'Holloway Girl' (Hogarth/Rothery/Kelly/Trewavas/Mosley)
A phased, scratchily picked bass riff leads off the tale of Judith Ward, a young woman who was sentenced to life in prison in 1974 after she confessed to bombing a bus carrying off-duty British soldiers and their families. Ward suffered from delusions and other mental illness, and in taking responsibility for the attack, the Irish Republican Army averred she had no connection to the group. Nevertheless, she was convicted and sentenced to life imprisonment, a sentence only overturned in 1992 as 'a grave miscarriage of justice.'

In Hogarth's hands, the story becomes one of perseverance in the face of injustice. The verses, in A minor, are dark and difficult, but the D-mixolydian choruses explode into hopeful affirmation: 'One day freedom will unlock your door.' The bass line repeats through it all, obstinate and unchanging, refusing to give in no matter how much changes around it. The key changes again for a guitar solo and bridge, then returns to D for a final long chorus, which crashes away to leave just the bass that began the track, still scratching away, perhaps forever.

'Berlin' (Hogarth/Rothery/Kelly/Trewavas/Mosley/Helmer)
Despite being about 'the mascara'd blonde from the Berliner bar,' this song has nothing to do with Fish's wife – in fact, Steve Rothery told John Helmer nothing about Marillion's time in Berlin, only that the music had tried to capture the atmosphere of the city. The lyric tells the tale of a young man who tries to escape to West Berlin to reunite with said blonde, 'a Berlin party girl,' only to be shot in no-man's land for his troubles. It's one of John's best, featuring some particularly cutting phrases – the shooting, for example, is given as 'dancing in the spotlight to the sound of clapping hands.'

It begins with a soft, slightly delayed guitar arpeggio that carries under the first verses (sound familiar?) and a short sax solo. A bass run and drum build introduce the climactic second section – a sort-of chorus – which shifts view from the girl to her lover, caught mid-flight. Then it all drops away for a creaking bridge over a lone martial snare, building until the bass and synth hit together like faraway thunder and the guitar squeals.

Finally 'Berlin' comes alive with pounding kick drum, scratching power chords, echoing delay guitar, and sing-song lyric that becomes a dark incantation in Hogarth's voice: 'the butcher, the baker, the munitions maker/the overachiever, the armistice breaker...' This list of 'the quick and the dead' reels into a full-bore guitar solo, lurching between squealing high bends and rumbling low phrases, fading away with the band behind it into a single, orchestral synth wash over which Hogarth repeats the first plaintive lyric, now recast as the leftovers of an everyday tragedy.

'After Me' (Hogarth/Rothery/Kelly/Trewavas/Mosley)
Like 'Going Under,' the B-side of 'Hooks in You' appears on *Seasons End* as a CD-only, mid-album bonus track. The reason for excluding it is obvious when placed against 'Easter,' which begins with the same twelve-string guitar, at the same tempo, in the same time, playing almost the exact same changes. Nevertheless, it's a charming love song, full of thoughtful imagery from Hogarth ('there's a heart on her sleeve from a spill of red wine') and an attentive arrangement.

After the refrain the song changes from pre-Marillion Hogarth to lively prog, dropping to an unexpected minor tonality with a chiming keyboard figure under which the band builds to a sudden crashing bridge that, rather than back away, just builds upon itself, becoming more and more intense – via stacked guitars, rolling drums, even a tremolo-picked bass line – as it fades.

'Hooks in You' (Hogarth/Rothery/Kelly/Trewavas/Mosley/Helmer)
Every band has a song like this: wildly outside their style, but too good not to release. Excepting a few bars of 7/8 in the intro and solo, 'Hooks in You' is a straight-ahead rock song in every aspect. Hogarth's goofy lyric describes a predatory woman from the position of the worried friend of her latest prey; Ian and Pete play the driving eighth-note beat with a straight face; Steve sweeps and tremolo-picks his way through the squealing fills. There's nothing prog about it, certainly nothing Marillion other than the excellent musicianship, which recalls the *Jurassic Park*

quip that they were 'so preoccupied with whether or not they *could*, they didn't stop to think if they *should*.'

And yet – it's a terrific little song.

(A historical footnote: Marillion's long-time festival pals Iron Maiden also featured an unusually poppy, but terrific, song called 'Hooks in You' on 1990's *No Prayer for the Dying* – their first with guitarist Janick Gers, who had just finished work on Fish's debut record.)

'The Space...' (Hogarth/Rothery/Kelly/Trewavas/Mosley/Woore/Dugmore/Harper)

The finale to *Seasons End* is a challenging song that proved Hogarth could go as dark as Fish. A paean to human alienation, Hogarth takes his central metaphor from a strange scene: 'I once saw an Amsterdam tram rip the side off a parked car which had been left too near the tramlines. It did so without slowing down. In terms of mass, the competition was so one-sided, like a ball-bearing and a feather, that I often wonder whether the tram driver noticed it happen. The damage was massive, inevitable, and casual. It's an enduring memory. I have occasionally been the tram. And I have often been the car.'

A chugging string section fades in and marches along beneath the first verse. The second verse hits like the proverbial tram it describes, bringing in the full band around the strings. This dynamic carries through a pre-chorus; when the chorus hits, the strings drop away in favour of layered guitars and a tripping keyboard figure. The post-chorus, recalling the verse, brings the strings back in, while keeping the band at full blast.

A very Rothery bridge follows, the rhythm section backing off as multiple guitars play interlocking delayed lines. The string section swells slowly beneath it until the drums beat back in for a rolling 3/4, military but syncopated. A synth chorus joins in under a short guitar solo, then all dies off for the long outro, first just Hogarth's voice over a pad, delivering the message of the song: 'Everybody in the whole of the world/feels the same inside.' The second pass through is heralded by a low synth sweep and buoyed by the return of the drums, playing a slow, deep-pocketed, almost swung 4/4, the snare hits snapping like gunshots. Guitar fills rise and retreat around Hogarth's straining voice, which is the last man left standing on a stretched final note after the band hits their last hit... until a single low tom, sunk in a long tail of reverb, hits a thunderclap to close out the album.

(Another historical aside: the lengthy songwriting credits to 'The

Space…' arose in 1994 from legal action on the part of Steve Hogarth's old The Europeans bandmates – the verse melody came from an unreleased Europeans song called 'So Far Away,' while the long outro was based on another tune, 'Wrap Me in the Flag.' Or as Hogarth later quipped, 'I put my words and melody onto some chords that Mark had already written, but Colin [Woore] said the chords were his chords and they were too precious too him to be released.')

'The Bell in the Sea' (B-side of 'The Uninvited Guest', Hogarth/Rothery/Kelly/Trewavas/Mosley/Helmer)

Palm-muted delay guitar fades in over a symphonic synth arrangement to introduce this tune inspired by a Whitby legend of a church bell that, being transported by sea, sank during a shipwreck. The gentle rise of the introduction crashes suddenly into a new key (from C# minor down to B minor) and a clangourous verse/chorus arrangement. The bridge, down in F# minor, is whispering and spooky – 'no one ever dreams and lives…' – then drops again to E for another bridge, which itself roars back to the verse groove in the introductory C#, before a snappy, structural guitar solo blazes away through the fadeout.

'The Release' (B-side of 'Easter', Hogarth/Rothery/Kelly/Trewavas/Mosley)

A squealing guitar sweeps up into Mark's triumphal keyboard chime over band hits, which roll into a shuffling, almost danceable uptempo for the verses. Hogarth's straightforward lyric makes a terrific love song: 'at the end of the day, you're the one who burns it all away.' Musically 'The Release' never strays from G major, the verses given an especially simple I-IV-V progression, while the arrangement keeps its manic energy from start to finish. Simple, perhaps, but fitting for this tribute to mutual support, treating mature love as rapturously as the brand-new kind.

Seasons End, and Hogarth, received wide-ranging reactions from press and fans. Mick Wall claimed in *Kerrang!* that 'you can almost forget the band ever had another singer' and *Sounds* called it 'the best record Marillion have made,' while *Spiral Scratch* had 'reservations about the ability of the new outfit to justify the name Marillion.' Meanwhile, some fans loved the new album while others gave up on the band entirely. John Arnison summed up the split, which hit Marillion hardest in their strongholds: 'We lost the heavy metal side of the fans. We never really got as big again in the UK or Germany.'

Unsurprisingly, there was no shortage of blame for Hogarth, who was pilloried in some corners as too cute, too pop, too mainstream. Nonetheless Marillion had a continent to re-conquer under their new flag. The tour began 5 October in front of some 10,000 people in Besancon, France and continued with shows almost every day across Europe before winding up at Le Zenith in Paris for the capstone show.

'Each gig,' Mark recalled, 'it was like, that's it, we've won that audience over... everywhere we went, especially the key dates like Paris and the first London show that we did at the Astoria.' Added Ian, 'Paris was the biggest gig for Steve on that particular leg of the tour... I think that was the point where Steve really had to deliver the goods as a frontman.' It featured an important moment for Hogarth, as well:

[I]t got towards the end of the show and I thanked the audience for being so supportive of this first time out and they just made this noise that wouldn't stop ... [T]he show stopped for what seemed like a long time but probably was only two or three minutes, and I looked round at the band and the band were as stunned as I was, because I don't think any of the five of us had experienced anything like it. This noise just went up and the whole place was screaming and shaking. And I couldn't talk over it, and they wouldn't stop! And it wasn't the end of the show, it was just, I was trying to introduce the next song.

That first London show took place two weeks later, on 7 November, marking Marillion's first proper show in the UK with Hogarth at the helm. Fish meanwhile had spent the entire stretch of Marillion's continental tour blanketing Scotland and England, with a show nearly every day from 11 October to 12 November. 'State of Mind,' the lead single from his upcoming debut, released on 16 October despite the album being months away. Its trajectory paralleled that of 'Hooks in You' almost perfectly: it entered the charts at #32 on 28 October, fell to #36, hung on at #58, then exited after three weeks. It seemed that neither act would simply be handed the reception they'd fought so hard for together.

Following Hogarth's London debut it was off to America, to play a show each in New York City and Los Angeles. 'Hooks in You' made a fleeting appearance on the Billboard Mainstream Rock chart during the visit, just three weeks with a peak of #49 on 18 November. Then, as the band rested up before their proper UK run, the second single from *Seasons End* appeared in the form of 'The Uninvited Guest' on 27 November. Despite a much more cinematic video, featuring Hogarth leering at himself from a floating chair and some horror-film lighting, it barely registered on the charts, with a #53 entry on 9 December and just one more week at #60.

The UK gigs had no trouble converting old fans, though, at twelve shows between the 3 December kickoff in Newcastle and the closer at the Hammersmith Odeon on the 18th. Despite having had a chance to settle in across the Channel, Hogarth was still all nerves when confronted with Marillion's original fanbase. 'I thought I'd get nailed, I really did think I'd get nailed,' he told a TV interviewer afterwards, 'and I was a nervous wreck at the first couple of shows, and I was especially nervous up at the Glasgow Barrowlands.' He would again be pleasantly surprised by the ebullience with which Marillion's fans welcomed him – long-time fan Paul Hughes said of the Barrowlands, 'From the moment H came on stage the crowd was behind him, and there was a real magical feeling of rebirth in the room. I went home with my confidence renewed.'

The eighties closed with the release on 27 December of Fish's second single, the driving hard rock, blaring horns, and America-critical lyric of 'Big Wedge.' It outperformed both Fish's and Marillion's efforts thus far, though not by much, entering at #26 on 6 January, peaking at #25 the next week, and holding on for two more weeks. But it remained to be seen how *Seasons End* would stack up against the ex-singer's debut, which EMI had sat on for a full six months and only now, as the nineties loomed, would see fit to release.

1990-2020: Such an Amazing Thing

Marillion spent 1990 largely on the road, showing the flag in every corner of their fandom to keep old fans on board and try to win new ones. The tour began on 27 January with the biggest show Steve Hogarth had ever played, a co-headliner with Bon Jovi at the Hollywood Rock Festival in Rio de Janeiro. Some 80,000 fans came out, making the new singer an instant star in Brazil.

Late January was even more momentous for Fish, as his solo debut *Vigil in a Wilderness of Mirrors* was finally released on the 29th. Like *Seasons End*, *Vigil* was promptly certified silver thanks to solid presales, but both camps would have to wait until the 10 February charts to discover that Fish had outranked his former colleagues with a #5 entrance. The victory soon seemed little more than a fluke, however, as again events suggested that perhaps Fish and Marillion had been better off together than apart. *Vigil* followed the same trajectory as *Seasons End*, slipping to #25, then sliding for just three more weeks as February turned into March.

Vigil in a Wilderness of Mirrors

Personnel:
Fish (Derek W. Dick): vocals
Frank Usher: guitars (Tracks 1-7 and 9)
Hal Lindes: guitars (1-7)
Janick Gers: guitars (8)
John Giblin: bass guitars (1-9)
Mickey Simmonds: keyboards (1-9)
Davy Spillane: pipes (1), whistles (1)
Phil Cunningham: whistles (1 and 4), accordion (4), bodhrán (4)
Aly Bain: violin (4)
Gavyn Wright: violin (4)
Mark Brzezicki: drums (1, 2, 4, 6-9)
John Keeble: drums (3)
Luís Jardim: percussion (2-4 and 9)
Carol Kenyon: backing vocals (2, 3, 7 and 9)
Tessa Niles: backing vocals (2, 7 and 9)
Jon Kelly: producer
Release date: 29 January 1990
Highest chart places: 5 (UK)
Running time: 46:32 (LP), 51:18 (CD)

If *Seasons End* was hampered by a lack of sonic variety, Fish's solo
debut suffers from the opposite problem. It ranges widely in style and
production, resulting in something that sounds less like a coherent
statement than a shotgun approach to hitmaking. It's also a far cry from
anything Fish put out with Marillion – depending on how one defines
'prog,' *Vigil* is hardly a prog record at all aside from the title track. Still,
progressive rock is a big tent, the individual songs are strong, and the
production and musicianship by Jon Kelly and a band of studio players
are excellent. It's no wonder that *Vigil* remains Fish's most successful, and
one of his best loved, solo efforts.

The title references a phrase that entered public consciousness via
the mid-century CIA Counterintelligence chief James Jesus Angleton,
who borrowed the term 'wilderness of mirrors' from T.S. Eliot's poem
'Gerontion' to describe the confusion of disinformation in espionage.
(Ironically, Angleton himself was disgraced following the revelation of his
own mass surveillance of segments of the American public.) From him,
it was taken up by writers of espionage novels and non-fiction, including
Spycatcher by Peter Wright, where Fish found it. The vigil, however, is
Fish's own.

'Vigil' (Dick/Simmonds)

The album begins with something of a sop to Marillion fans: a prog mini-
epic with rich arranging and dark, abstract lyrics. It sets an expectation
that the rest of the album doesn't really match, but perhaps it rendered
listeners more open-minded to what would come next.

The lyric, expanding the 'Voice in the Crowd' theme, drips with
disillusionment and cynicism. Fish describes a world where actions and
consequences are unhooked, 'even the good guys must die,' and his only
chance is to 'keep a vigil in a wilderness of mirrors' to seek out the truth
that may rescue him. There are snatches of irony, too – the very first lyric
is 'Listen to me, just hear me out/if I could have your attention,' a neat
opener to a debut solo album.

Musically, 'Vigil' comprises numerous unique sections. Its opening
incantation is delivered softly over a reverb-drenched synth pulse, layering
in a few subtle flourishes, until Fish's voice leaps up an octave to belt
out the song's core plaint: 'I don't know the score anymore/it's not clear
anymore.'

Next comes the verse with a delayed guitar gallop, picking up the pace
and amplifying the paranoia. Gunshot-like drum hits keep wide-open

time, then roll into the pre-chorus and chorus, leaping to a major tonality with big hits and a thumping bass as Fish begs for assistance and declares his vigil. A martial snare rattle and whining Scottish-folk pipes mark a return to darkness for a long instrumental middle. Another verse follows, the arrangement more agitated than the first, making the resolution to the pre-chorus that much greater a relief.

The final chorus pulls a neat trick, extending itself not by simply playing again but adding a short double-time build between repetitions, then a short coda to bring the whole dynamic down again until we're left with a reprise of the intro, wondering whether Fish really learned anything at all.

'Big Wedge' (Dick/Simmonds)

The best of *Vigil*'s singles opens with a drum roll and a blast of horns. Funky bass locks with a driving beat and a clangy guitar to push Fish's excoriation of American money culture. The lyric is of a piece with other rock songs of the time, kicking back against the politicians and televangelists who got rich stirring up moral panic over pop lyrics. (As an example, Iron Maiden's 'Holy Smoke' features a similar theme – and, like 'Hooks in You,' appeared on 1990's *No Prayer for the Dying*.)

It's not Fish at his most elegant – 'You see him coast to coast on live TV/ in a stadium rocked by Satan just the night before' isn't exactly subtle – but the words flow nicely over the snappy drums and pounding bass. The chorus is especially fun, with blaring horn fills and layered gang vocals. The only jarring moment is the bridge, which smartly puts a rattling lid on the song's energy, but features Fish speak-singing with such sour tuning that one wonders whether Jon Kelly was out sick the day they tracked the vocal. Still, it's broken up by a quirky, shreddy guitar solo, and quick enough to get back to a final set of variations on the glorious chorus.

'State of Mind' (Dick/Lindes/Simmonds)

The lead single, featuring Spandau Ballet drummer John Keeble on the kit, is a jazzy number based off one of Fish's early political lyrics, not far from the message of 'Vigil' – the world is screwed up, Fish is having a breakdown about it, but maybe humanity can cut through the noise together.

It opens with a funky bass shuffle in E mixolydian, with layered percussion and a few faraway guitar fills and swells moving things along until Fish enters, soft and reverby. Things pick up for the singalong chorus ('We the people are gettin' tired of being tired!') with a proud E major tonality, electric guitar hits, and the full drum kit, though the bass keeps its groove going. The second verse and chorus follow the same dynamic, leading into a snappy acoustic guitar solo over an even more stripped back verse arrangement. Fish returns with just the back half of a third verse, then a final chorus into an outro that loops back to the beginning.

Overall, 'State of Mind' is remarkably understated, perhaps too much so. But if Fish was trying to reframe himself as a Phil Collins figure, moving from success with an arcane prog band into intelligent, modern pop, it was a logical choice for his reintroduction.

'The Company' (Dick/Simmonds)

The original lyric for 'The Company' was written after a meeting between Fish and Bob Ezrin in 1988, just before the split with Marillion. Ezrin told Fish to go off and write a drinking song, and the singer produced a ominous account of his relationship with the band – which is also a drinking song. The bridge says it all: 'The sooner you realise I'm perfectly happy/if I'm left to decide the company I choose...'

Piano, strings, and folk instruments take the lead over a boozy 6/8 swing, only occasionally interrupted by ominous electric guitars, sticking to a gloomy D minor other than a brief pass through the relative major in the chorus, a sort of nod-and-wink to the idea that maybe this is just a harmless drinking song after all.

After the second chorus is an instrumental break, a sort of folk orchestra playing through the chorus like an ancient Scots racial memory, but it only gets one pass before it's totally overpowered by the return of the lush, soaring strings and hard-hit drums. Then the strings get their own break, all baroque and dripping with honey, before the bridge pulls us into a beautifully-arranged half verse and a long, soaring chorus. It's tempting to read the instrumentation as a reflection of Fish's own battle between his middle-class Scots roots and the gold-plated fame of the music biz, a theme he would explore further on his follow-up *Internal Exile* – but if that goes too far, it's still a master class in rock orchestration.

'A Gentleman's Excuse Me' (Dick/Simmonds)

Though it didn't chart as well as 'Big Wedge,' this pleading ballad has proved Fish's most lasting solo tune. From the swelling strings and plinking piano to the lyrics full of paper flowers, fairy tales, and gipsy dancers, 'A Gentleman's Excuse Me' is almost painfully saccharine – yet somehow it works.

Partially that's thanks to the unexpected depth of the lyric, which like 'Kayleigh' before it is more than just a broken-hearted love song. Fish calls his ex-lover out for holding onto an impossible fantasy rather than putting in the effort to make a real relationship work – thus proving how intimately he knows her, while simultaneously offering up some tough love. It's the sort of challenge you can only make to someone who's put her heart in your hands in the past.

But the song also succeeds musically. The melody is singable by mortals, avoiding the heights of Fish's range as well as its gnarlier tones. The arrangement – just piano, strings, and horns – is vulnerable and prideful in equal measures, switching back and forth as needed. The vocal sometimes rides it like a wave, other times sinks in like bare feet on a plush carpet.

It's a thoughtful song disguised as a simple one all the way to the end, when the final chorus resolves not back to its usual F major, but the relative D minor, a sudden stab of melancholy as Fish admits that he's failed to win his love back: 'We're finished dancing.'

'The Voyeur (I Like to Watch)' (Dick/Simmonds)

The B-side of 'State of Mind,' 'The Voyeur' is another CD-only track. It's another from the Phil Collins school of funky, tight pop rock, opening with an electric piano riff like 'Superstition' on cocaine, fast and hard to follow. Massive drums pin the riff down with a hammering 6/8, and Fish keeps a constrained vocal range for the verse, delivering an indictment of television culture that's no more subtle than the rest of the record.

The clutch opens up for the chorus, the bass going full gallop as the drums add slithering cymbals to really get things moving, all over an unexpected Bb major. This dynamic is only slightly restrained in the second verse, breaking out again for the next chorus – with new lyrics, a nice touch – then dropping everything but the kit for a metronomic break into the bridge.

Inexplicably fluting synths twitter around Fish's voice, recasting the groove as a sort of fairy dance, then Fish's real motive is revealed: 'the world will know my name,' he declares to the tolling of a bell, the voyeur desperate to get in on the action. The verse kicks back in for a roaring organ solo, and the drums carry through a final chorus and into a long outro full of squealing guitar stabs and layered mutterings until two final drum hits shut the proceedings down.

'Family Business' (Dick/Lindes/Simmonds)

A slow, sinister song of abuse and cover-up, 'Family Business' is cleverly placed right after 'Voyeur' – this time it's no fun peering into other people's lives, just an awkward tragedy. The tune is built around a crawling minor progression in a mid-tempo 6/8, carried mainly by a simple piano arpeggio and slippery bass. The drums get more active for the chorus, tapping out a tricky cymbal pattern around a hollow snare backbeat, but everything stays restrained – the narrator, keeping the bad news inside.

The tension builds across the second verse, which is graced with a new prechorus featuring a chugging palm-muted electric guitar, which returns in the second chorus with sobbing harmonized fills. Release is offered by a brief major-key shift in the instrumental bridge, all stacked guitars that build and collapse, rise and fall, but the minor tonality is inescapable. The third verse barely backs off, and the pre-chorus that follows ratchets things back up to full before the last chorus.

The song ends with a fourth verse, as muted as the first, in which Fish realises that by staying silent, he's as responsible as anyone for the cycle of abuse that carries on next door. But the crisis of the moment has passed and things have calmed just enough to be survivable for everyone involved; all that's left is the grim realisation that if nobody steps up and says something, the cycle will repeat forever.

'The View from the Hill' (Dick/Gers)

Co-written with soon-to-be Iron Maiden guitarist Janick Gers, 'The View from the Hill' is something like Fish's version of a hair-metal power ballad. The lyrics, not exactly subtle about Fish's experience of the music industry, tackle the album's running motif of the hill, an eternal climb for fame and money as well as a tottering pile of discarded junk.

As a song, it's a bit uneven, full of interesting moments that don't quite fit together. It begins with some very Queensrÿche harmonised acoustic guitar and Fish's voice at its loosest and bluesiest – not a bad place for him, but a bit of a mismatch with the rigid lyrics ('You can't see the wood for the trees, 'cause the forest is burning/and you say it's the smoke in your eyes that's making you cry'). Things pick up with the entry of a palm-muted heavy chug – pure metal – which lead to a wordy sort of chorus straight out of the eighties Deep Purple playbook: 'You were a dancer and a chancer, a poet and a fool,' Fish snarls over crashing guitars, 'to the royalty of mayhem you were breaking all the rules.'

This falls back into the softer verse, though with more involved drumming, which chugs its way back into another slashing chorus (with totally different lyrics). An instrumental break reimagines the intro as massive electric guitar hits, then rolls into a fleet-fingered solo from Gers that one can imagine him including on his Iron Maiden audition tape. A third chorus crashes in (with a third set of lyrics), then finally the outro refigures the intro again, this time with a proper beat to drive it and a mass of guitars and synths piling up like the beautiful garbage pile on the cover of the album, until the whole thing collapses under its own weight and only a lone acoustic guitar survives.

'Cliché' (Dick/Lindes/Simmonds)

The album closer is easily its weakest song, an interminable ballad with awkward, ill-fitted lyrics that's only partially redeemed by some creative guitar from ex-Dire Straits player Hal Lindes. 'I've got a reputation of being a man with a gift of words,' Fish begins, undermining himself right off the bat. This one needed an editor – the overwritten lyrics don't sit in the groove, forcing Fish to rush or stretch to fit in his lines, suggesting that words and music were written separately and stuck together in the studio.

Musically, the song starts with a simple minor-key piano, chiming guitar harmonics, and a hi-hat keeping time. The drums kick in after the first verse, as does a snaky but simple guitar line that drops out all too soon when the second verse begins. Luckily it returns for the chorus, bringing some interest to the empty spaces between Fish's refrain.

The bridge keeps up the pace while changing up the chords, but there's no saving the next block of lyrics: 'It's not that I'm embarrassed or shy, well you know me too well/But I want to make this song special in a way that you can tell/That it's solely for you, and for nobody else/For my best friend, my lover, when I need help – cliché.' Well, yes, a lot of them – and somebody should have told Fish.

Hal's bendy, reverbed-out guitar solo is next, and it's a pretty nice one. The song's groove works well with the right lead, and the dynamics rise and fall appealingly. There's another bridge after that, then another sort-of bridge that peels back the arrangement until it's little more than a shuffling drum kit as Fish avers that 'the best way' is 'an old cliché: I love you.'

And that's it – except it's not. The song ends, then restarts with a big boomy drum fill and a melodramatic key change. In a more engaging song, or maybe one that wasn't seven minutes long, it would be a cool trick, but here we just end up getting the same bridge we've already heard, only higher. Then the refrain, many times, with some soulful guitar fills snaking around it and, at last, a raking mini-guitar solo to lead us out.

'Jack and Jill' (B-side of 'Big Wedge,' Dick/Simmonds)

One of Fish's most Marillion-sounding tracks, 'Jack and Jill' begins with a lush, simple C-major synth line rising and falling under guitar feedback. The verses, soft and open, move through some unexpected chord changes before crashing back into big open guitar chords (nicked from The Who) for the chorus. The whole repeats, then the intro synth returns at double speed, jumps up a step, then another half step for an accelerated chorus – then dumps back to the original key and leaps back and forth between that and D for a long outro guitar solo. The whole second half of the song is a blast, flashy and fun, and would have made a great album track.

Ten years later, Fish bemoaned what he saw as poor handling of *Vigil* by EMI. 'I honestly think that if the "Vigil..." album had been a Marillion album, it would've been even bigger,' he told *Classic Rock* magazine. 'But EMI asked me to delay it because they wanted Marillion's album out first. They said they'd give it full promotion, da da da ... Three years is a long time. It was difficult to pull the fans back in again. It was a lot easier for Marillion, because they had the name and the EMI press people always focused on them.'

The singer would go on to understand the financial problems that mounted through the nineties as stemming from the decision-making around *Vigil*. After recording it, he'd already launched one UK tour in late 1989, but touring took money: 'The finances quickly dwindled away as the reality of supporting session musicians, equipping a demo studio and touring rig and all the rest of the necessary paraphernalia used to ready a band from scratch took its toll.' Thus Fish began the nineties in the hole, and in addition, he'd now gone a full year without any advance from EMI, who were waiting to see how *Vigil* fared before exercising their option for a follow-up. Still, the album was finally out, and he intended to support it properly.

Marillion spent February in a circuit of Canada and the US. Returning to the small clubs of their inaugural US tour in 1983 may have felt like slumming it after Rio, but sadly didn't pay off in either record sales or venue upgrades. In March it was back to continental Europe for another spin through the strongholds of France and Germany. Fish kicked off his own tour at the same time, supporting his third single, 'A Gentleman's Excuse Me.' The single was released on the 5th and did about as well as 'Hooks in You' and 'State of Mind' – a #30 entry on the 17th, then two more weeks on the charts – as Fish and Marillion both trod the stages of Europe. (The night of 12 March, French fans could choose to see either Fish in Paris or Marillion outside Bordeaux. Germany had their pick on both the 22nd and 24th.)

EMI fired the last bullet in its gun only two weeks after 'A Gentleman's Excuse Me,' with 'Easter,' the third single from *Seasons End*, hitting shelves on cassette on 19 March. (The 7", 12", and CD singles came a week later.) 'Easter' earned only two weeks on the charts in mid-April, at #34 on the 14th (the day before the holiday for which it was named) and #35 the week after. Thus the two much-anticipated new albums came and went, alongside three singles each. Despite dual Top 10 placements, sales in this new era looked thin when contrasted with the high water mark of Marillion's previous two releases.

Both acts toured into April, then resumed in June for the festival season (and another stab at America by Marillion). While neither had met EMI's high expectations, it was Fish whose relationship with the label was being tested. Despite selling well – his run wrapped with a sold-out show at the Royal Albert Hall in London on 9 July – this leg of the tour had lost even more money for the singer. He recalled,

> I took a gamble that within the year I could reach the audience numbers I had gotten accustomed to with Marillion... In short I'd been away too long and the fallout from the messy divorce [had] alienated a lot of fans. I went for an expensive concert production in order to impress the media and crowds that I was still a 'big time' act. The gigs sold well but the costs were too high and the expected return to touring larger venues in the Summer [sic] and thereby recouping our losses didn't happen.

Further, he said, 'I expected EMI to support another single and grease the wheels of the touring bandwagon.' And indeed, *Vigil* had done well enough that the label deemed a follow-up warranted, but they offered Fish the same contract as before. Deep in the hole after months on the road, Fish found the offered advance 'barely enough to cover recording costs never mind my personal needs.'

So he went to court, gambling on his lawyers' promises that EMI would back down and make a better offer rather than take the case all the way to the High Court. He lost, and soon discovered that not only could he not afford a High Court trial, but the court had hit him with an injunction preventing him from releasing any music until the case was settled. Now not only was the bridge with EMI burned, no other label would pick Fish up, on the chance that he would ultimately lose to EMI and be forbidden from releasing whatever he'd recorded in the meantime.

Marillion's relationship with EMI was much happier, at least for the moment. They would go on to record three more studio records for the label, though these would fail to surpass *Seasons End*, let alone resurrect the band's golden years.

1991's *Holidays in Eden*, the first written entirely with Hogarth and an intentional stab at a commercial sound with a number of made-for-radio tracks, would repeat *Seasons End*'s #7 debut. Its three singles all landed in the same mid-30s range as the last trio, and when Marillion under Hogarth finally broke the Top 20 the next year, it was with a cover of 'Sympathy' by Rare Bird, a non-album track that reached #17 but faded quickly.

In 1994 Marillion swung back towards their prog-rock roots with the concept album *Brave*, which became an instant fan favourite, but they'd been too long out of the spotlight of a changing music industry to have much impact on the charts. *Brave* landed at #10 and slipped away in a month. Nevertheless, its impact on music was felt soon after on Radiohead's breakthrough album *OK Computer*, which shared production techniques and songwriting similarities with *Brave*. (No coincidence, perhaps, that the earliest known photograph of Radiohead prominently features the fold-out poster from Marillion's 'Farewell to '83' Christmas tour program, which was only available at five shows.)

Meanwhile Fish trod an even rockier road. After a long and bitter fight with EMI he was picked up by Polydor for the follow-up. *Internal Exile* arrived at the end of 1991, packed with a potent mix of Scottish-nationalist folk rock and hard-hitting prog and featuring production and engineering by Chris Kimsey and Thomas Stiehler of *Misplaced Childhood*. But without the Marillion name or advertising budget, it was a hard sell to the British public: the album landed at #21 at the start of November and was gone before the month was out. (Fish has also attributed the album's cold reception by English fans and reviewers to its strong Scottish-nationalist direction.)

Fish finished out his obligation to Polydor in 1993 with a covers album, *Songs from the Mirror*. The singer has mostly disowned *Mirror*, saying he did it so that Polydor wouldn't take the money and run if he gave them the strong material he'd cooked up for his next album, but in fact it's a terrific collection. The song choices are familiar yet interesting, the arrangements walk the line between faithful and fresh, and Fish's voice is showcased admirably as he breaks out of his usual mould.

Songs from the Mirror only reached #46 upon release, and Polydor didn't offer Fish a new contract. Rather than go begging again, and spurred by a session with a spiritual medium in which the singer's grandfather spoke to him, Fish struck out on his own. In 1994, the newly established Dick Bros Record Company released *Suits* – musically a contender for Fish's best solo album, *Suits* also outdid both *Internal Exile* and *Mirror* with a #20 chart entry.

1995 marked Marillion's last studio album for EMI, *Afraid of Sunlight*. Suffering from a lack of promotion, it reached only #16 at the head of a three-week stay. After thirteen years, the time had finally come to bid EMI farewell. The next year's live album *Made Again* marked the band's final EMI release, a mercy since it both fulfilled Marillion's five-album contract with EMI and earned enough to pay off the debts still owed from the over-the-top production of *Brave*.

In the lurch, Marillion signed with Castle Communications, a small label known mostly for reissues and compilations that had struck out into original heavy metal with the Raw Power imprint. They landed a three-album deal, but upon the 1997 release of *This Strange Engine* the band discovered that Red Ant, their US distributor, had dissolved and they couldn't afford to mount a North American tour.

This necessity became the mother of an invention that would change the world.

Ten years after their last Top 5 album, Marillion had been abandoned by their label and the press, but not their fans. Across the Atlantic, a disheartened American named Jeff Pelletier hatched a scheme. On Marillion's budding internet message boards he posted a simple plea to his fellow Freaks: 'If you want to see Marillion – send money.'

Fans from all over responded in droves, depositing donations into a bank account Pelletier set up. 'People were giving money just to see this happen, because it was such an amazing thing,' he recalled. As Marillion watched in disbelief, the so-called Tour Fund exploded. 'Once it got past the $25,000 mark,' recalled Mark, 'we started making plans for the tour.' The Tour Fund eventually hit some $47,000 and funded a 21-date tour. It was a huge moment for Marillion, proving the power and dedication of their fanbase, but its impact would be felt far beyond the world of prog rock: Jeff Pelletier had invented internet crowdfunding.

The same year, Fish released his fourth studio album, *Sunsets on Empire*, via Dick Bros. Despite charting at #42, *Sunsets* was a bank-breaking flop for Fish. The record undersold expectations and the tour even more so, bankrupting Dick Bros and putting the singer into nearly a million pounds of debt. Perhaps spurred by these losses (as well as *Best of Both Worlds*, a split Fish-Hogarth compilation released by EMI in 1997), he approached Marillion around this time about doing a joint tour, with each band performing separately then joining together to perform *Misplaced Childhood*. The band rejected his advances, but the final refusal came from Fish: 'Arnison came back to me and said, "Come out without your band, Marillion'll learn some of your solo stuff." I declined because it'd look like I was going back to Marillion.'

Nevertheless, 1997 had a final surprise in store for Fish and Marillion alike: on the back of EMI's remastered CD reissues, both *Script for a Jester's Tear* and *Seasons End* earned new sales certifications on 5 December. *Seasons End* was certified gold and *Script* finally hit platinum, fourteen years after its debut.

1998 opened with two breaks: one from the treadmill of touring and recording, and the other with long-time manager John Arnison. Marillion's inaugural email newsletter in February announced the split in the usual bland language: 'things change and our vision and his were no longer one-and-the-same.'

But behind the scenes, not only had Arnison seemingly given up on the band – he suggested they all consider it a part-time gig going forward – but Fish's dark accusations were seemingly vindicated as Arnison resisted giving Marillion full access to their financials. 'John seemed to adopt a policy of "deliberate vagueness,"' as Steve drily put it. Arnison was out, temporarily replaced with Iron Maiden manager Rod Smallwood. Eventually, Lucy Jordache of EMI, a long-time Marillion devotee, would take the reins, a position she still holds today.

Marillion did two more records with Castle, 1998's *Radiation* and 1999's *marillion.com*. Appropriately for a record that celebrated their internet fanbase, *marillion.com* was actually released on the band's new self-owned label Intact, and only distributed by Castle – but also marked a darker milestone as the first Marillion album to fail to break the UK Top 40, charting for only one week at #53. Fish's own 1999 release *Raingods with Zippos*, despite being picked up by Roadrunner Records, met a similar fate: a single week at #57.

With their obligation to Castle fulfilled, Marillion had hit their nadir. 'It certainly felt like things were going down,' Mark recalled, 'and didn't show any signs of stopping.' Facing a handful of unappealing offers from indie labels, the band opted instead for a leap of faith and struck out on their own with a groundbreaking project that took the lesson of the Tour Fund to a new level: crowdfunding an entire album from the ground up.

Recalled Hogarth of the Tour Fund, 'That really woke us up to two things. First, that the fans would do anything for us, and second, the internet would be a godsend ... We thought, if we can talk to them, if we know where they are, then we don't need a record label any more.' So an email went out to the band's mailing list, some 30,000 strong, asking if they'd be interested in pre-ordering an album that hadn't been recorded yet.

The response was swift: in two days Marillion had 6,000 preorders; within three weeks, enough money to fund the record. Ultimately some 12,000 fans pre-ordered *Anoraknophobia*, punningly named in honour of the fans themselves – analogous to 'geek' or 'otaku,' 'anorak' is British slang for an obsessive fan of a niche subject. The response was even enough to return Marillion briefly to the EMI fold with a worldwide marketing and distribution deal. (The *Anoraknophobia* campaign also featured incentives that are now all too familiar on Kickstarter, but were innovative at the time. A special edition CD with a bonus disc was sent to all who pre-ordered – and has never been reprinted – and those who got in early saw their names printed in a special thank-you list in the album notes.)

Fish also went indie again in the new millennium, releasing *Fellini Days* in 2001 on his new home label Chocolate Frog Records. *Field of Crows* followed, with mail-order sales in 2003 and a retail release in 2004, the same year as Marillion's *Marbles*.

Anorak energy had a much greater impact on the partially crowd-funded *Marbles* than just its presales. A vigorous fan campaign of calling and writing to radio stations resulted in the lead single, 'You're Gone,' entering the singles chart at #7 on 1 May 2004. It was Marillion's first song to chart since 'These Chains' from *Radiation* in 1998, and their first Top 10 since 'Incommunicado' in 1987.

The sudden popularity spurred BBC presenter Jonathan Ross to call them 'a prog rock band that sing about goblins,' at least according to Marillion's manager Lucy Jordache. (Steve Rothery got the last word: 'We recorded *Script for a Jester's Tear* 22 years ago. I think that was when Ross had his own hair.') The follow-up single, 'Don't Hurt Yourself,' hit #16, marking Hogarth's third Top 20 entry. *Anoraknophobia* and *Marbles* sold well, too, but neither was eligible for the album charts – both CD packages contained promotional stickers, which under the arcane rules of the Official Charts Company were considered a gift that could unfairly induce purchases.

By 2007 and their next studio album, *Somewhere Else*, Marillion didn't need pre-order money, and the traditionally-released record earned a #24 chart entry. (Hogarth has said the band would have felt guilty taking money when they didn't need it, but apparently the lack of a crowdfunding campaign disappointed many fans.)

Fish also put out a new record in 2007, *13th Star*, on Chocolate Frog. But the most noteworthy event of the year took place that summer at Hobble on the Cobbles, a free music festival in Aylesbury's market square, where Fish headlined. At the end of his set, he told the story of moving to Aylesbury in 1981 and befriending a 'lefty hero' named Brick who inspired a certain song called 'Market Square Heroes' – then introduced 'some old friends' in the form of Steve, Ian, Mark, and Pete to perform together for the first time in nearly twenty years. It was only one song, and has never been repeated, but it suggested that at last the hatchet had been buried.

2008's *Happiness is the Road* once again took preorders and once again didn't chart, though it did see the band duelling the shifting rules of the online music game. This time it was via peer-to-peer sharing services like Napster, where Marillion released files that appeared to be the album but in fact contained a video plea from the band, asking that would-be pirates either pay what they wanted or hand over an email address for a download.

It took until 2012 for Marillion to release their next album of original music, *Sounds That Can't Be Made*. This time online preorders didn't scuttle the record's chart position, as it reached a respectable #43 on 29 September. But the best was yet to come: after another four-year gap, *Fuck Everyone and Run* debuted at a stunning #4 on 6 October 2016.

Marillion's eighteenth studio album, and as of writing their most recent, remains Hogarth's best-ever showing, as well as outdoing both *Script for a Jester's Tear* and *Fugazi*. Nevertheless, the victory was bittersweet, as Hogarth explained: 'Record sales have fallen off a cliff due to downloading and streaming so a chart position is always tinged with a feeling of how many sales has it taken to get there... Any kind of chart position is a good thing mainly because it tends to wake the media up a bit and the phone starts ringing and everyone wants to talk to you.'

That media excitement led to Marillion's strongest reviews in years, as fans and press alike celebrated *FEAR*. No less an institution than *The Guardian* gave the album five stars and called it 'totally uncompromising,' 'as good as anything they have done,' and 'their best album in two decades.'

Fish's most recent album, as of writing, is also one of his finest. 2013's *A Feast of Consequences* features two achievements for Fish. One is 'Blind to the Beautiful,' a global-warming alarm produced in conjunction with Greenpeace and his first charting single since 1999, with a #36 placement on the UK Independent Singles chart. The other is a magnificent five-part suite inspired by World War I, a masterpiece of dark progressive songcraft.

Fish has one more album in the works, titled *Weltschmerz*, a German word meaning 'world-weariness.' It's an appropriate title from a man whose solo career has been burdened by disappointment and disaster, and for an album that was originally intended for a 2017 release but got pushed back numerous times. Recording was finally completed in early 2020, with an intended release in July – until, perhaps fittingly, the global COVID-19 pandemic delayed the record until late September. The accompanying tour played a single show in Aberdeen on Friday, 13 March before postponing all UK dates.

Marillion show no signs of stopping, especially following the glowing reception of *FEAR*. The band continues to keep their fans-first ethos alive, hosting wildly popular fan-club conventions and headlining prog festivals and cruises. In 2019 they undertook the 'With Friends from the Orchestra' tour, featuring orchestral rearrangements of classic songs spanning Hogarth's tenure with the band. A studio recording of these orchestral versions was released at the end of November. Nor has the band finished pushing the boundaries of music on the internet. December saw the return of the Marillion smartphone app and the launch of a dedicated video streaming service featuring live footage and documentaries.

In one way or another, Marillion has touched nearly every corner of the musical world. Radiohead may be the biggest band to show their influence, but they're far from the only one. Dream Theater, whose first live album was recorded at the Marquee Club, have inserted bits of 'Sugar Mice' into their own ballad 'Surrounded' and welcomed Rothery and Hogarth onstage for a rendition of 'Easter' during their famous covers show at Ronnie Scott's Jazz Club in 1995. Many younger progressive bands also reference Marillion, some pushing the envelope in their own right and others hearkening back to the early eighties days when the 'neo' in 'neo-prog' really meant something new. Then there are the numerous solo albums and tours, side projects, guest spots, and assorted miscellany put out by some of the hardest-working men in progressive music, all ensuring that Marillion's influence will be felt for generations to come.

Kay, Fish's hit-single muse, eventually reconnected with the singer who'd borrowed her name to find stardom. Despite more than twenty years having passed, for Fish, 'It was like I hadn't seen her for a week.' They rekindled their friendship, and after Kay told him she'd been diagnosed with cancer, Fish gave her a copy of *Misplaced Childhood*, which she'd never heard. Listening to it for the first time reduced her to tears – she had no idea how Fish had felt, nor just how much of the album was about her.

In the last year of her life, Kay took ownership of her act of inspiration and delighted in telling people she was the girl from the hit song. She died in October of 2012.

Diz Minnitt went on to play in another Aylesbury-based prog band, Pride of Passion, with Brian Jelleyman. He eventually became a social worker, earning acclaim helping youth offenders, and still goes by Diz.

Mick Pointer eventually landed on his feet in the music business. After more than a decade out of the game, he founded Arena with Clive Nolan of Pendragon in 1995. Arena went on to be a major neo-prog act of the nineties, but their inception was anything but auspicious, as Mick tells:

I was at McDonalds in Hemel Hempstead. There was a few guys in there with Marillion T shirts on who had just been to a Marillion gig in London. I said to these guys, 'was it a good gig' and they were all enthusiastic. I said to them basically, 'when you see the band, say hi to them for me' – they looked at me wondering who I was and I told them I was the reason they had Marillion on their T shirts. The penny dropped and they realised who I was. Anyway, one of those guys ran a prog rock fanzine who happened to know Clive Nolan and told him he's seen me and said he should write an album with me. Clive thought he'd never find me, but after phoning every kitchen design company in the Leighton Buzzard area, I was found and we set up a meeting... and still going strong.

Mick eventually reconnected with Doug Irvine, whom he invited to an Arena show in 2018. (There was no talk of the Silmarillion demo tapes Doug supposedly took.) The drummer has also met fan demand by touring the complete *Script for a Jester's Tear*, plus 'Grendel', as Mick Pointer's Script.

As far as that notorious fan favourite, Fish eventually played 'Grendel' live at a fan-club show in 2012. Steve gave in, too, with his Steve Rothery Band in 2019. By all accounts, Ian still hasn't learned it.